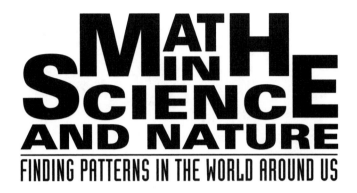

MATH IN SCIENCE AND NATURE

FINDING PATTERNS IN THE WORLD AROUND US

BY ROBERT GARDNER AND EDWARD A. SHORE

FRANKLIN WATTS
New York • Chicago • London • Toronto • Sydney

501.51
G176r

Photographs copyright ©: Visuals Unlimited: pp. 27 (John D.
Cunningham), 127 (Leonard Lee Rue III); Fundamental Photos: pp. 34,
35 (Richard Megna); Photo Researchers: pp. 55 (Dr. Tony Brain/SPL), 98
(Steve Kagan), 108 (John Spragens); Comstock/Russ Kinne: p. 65; Wide
World Photos: pp. 68, 77, 117; UPI/Bettmann: p. 71; Hal Jandorf: p.
115; Donald Brownlee, University of Washington: p. 119; NASA/JPL: p.
123.

Library of Congress Cataloging-in-Publication Data

Gardner, Robert, 1929–
    Math in science and nature : finding patterns in the world around
us / by Robert Gardner and Edward A. Shore.
    p.   cm.
    Includes index.
    ISBN 0-531-11196-2 (lib. bdg.)
    1. Mathematics—Juvenile literature.   2. Mathematics—Graphic
methods—Juvenile literature. [1. Mathematics.   2. Mathematics—
Graphic methods.]   I. Shore, Edward A.   II. Title.
QA40.5.G37   1994
501'.51—dc20   94-26878 CIP AC

CONTENTS

INTRODUCTION: THE SEARCH FOR ORDER AND PATTERNS

To the casual observer nature may seem chaotic, but one of the tasks of science is to search for order and patterns amid the seeming disorder. This is done by observing the world carefully, gathering data, and using the information accumulated to formulate generalizations or laws. Science also involves carrying out experiments and analyzing the data collected to answer questions and test hypotheses that arise in an attempt to explain all that goes on around us.

Mathematics has played a vital role in the human quest through science to understand the universe in which we live. As you will see, the patterns and generalizations extracted from nature can often be couched in mathematical terms. In this book, you will discover a few of nature's regularities and see the role that mathematics plays in codifying these patterns. We will also show you some of the mathematical methods you can use to search for regularities in nature.

USING THIS BOOK

In some sections of this book we will provide data and ask you to try to find patterns or relationships by applying mathematical analysis to the information. In other sections we will ask you to gather the data by carrying out investigations or exercises that require materials. To make such tasks easier, you will find a list of the things you will need to carry out the experiment or activity. We assume that you have access to and will use a pocket calculator for any calculations you are asked to make. We have also assumed that you have plenty of graph paper. In addition to regular graph paper, you will need semilog and log-log graph paper.

It will be a great help to have a notebook that you can use to write down the results of your experiments. It is usually best to record the results in tabular form. Graphs of your experimental results can be attached to pages of your notebook next to the tables of your results.

Experiments sometimes involve dangerous materials so you should always work safely. The following rules will serve as a guide.

SAFETY FIRST

- Any experiments should be done under the supervision of a teacher, a parent, or another knowledgeable adult.
- Read all instructions carefully. If you have questions, check with your supervisor. Don't take chances.
- Whether you work with a classmate, with a friend, or alone, maintain a serious attitude when experimenting. Horseplay can be dangerous to you and to others.
- Wear safety goggles whenever you are using anything that could damage your eyes.

- Keep flammable materials, such as alcohol, away from flames and other sources of heat.
- If you are using matches or flames, have a fire extinguisher and a fire blanket nearby and know how to use them.
- Keep the area where you are experimenting clean and organized.
- When you have finished, clean up and put away the materials you were using.
- Never experiment with the electricity in wall outlets except with the supervision of a knowledgeable adult.

1
USING MATHEMATICS IN SCIENCE

In this chapter you'll examine some of the basic mathematical tools and techniques that are used in science. You'll learn how to draw a variety of graphs and how to use these graphs to find patterns or relationships among the variables under investigation. In later chapters, you'll use these and other techniques to search for patterns or relationships in your own investigations or analyses.

DRAWING GRAPHS

Throughout this book you'll prepare and analyze graphs from data supplied to you or from data you'll obtain for yourself. You'll find it worthwhile to do the following activities first. They will help you to draw better graphs and to interpret the graphs that you analyze.

STRAIGHT-LINE GRAPHS
One kind of graph can be drawn using the data in Table 1. The data were obtained by measuring the mass in

Table 1: The Mass and Volume of Some Pieces of Copper

Mass (g)	Volume (cm^3)
32.1	3.6
50.0	5.6
64.5	7.2
11.0	1.2
20.8	2.3

grams and the volume in cubic centimeters of a number of different sized pieces of copper.

Plot a graph of the data by placing the mass numbers on the vertical axis and the volume numbers on the horizontal axis. Label each axis with the variable being represented and the units in which it was measured. In this case, the vertical axis will be labeled "mass (g)," and the horizontal axis "volume (cm^3)." Your graph should include one data point not listed in the table—the point at the origin (0 g, 0 cm^3) where the axes meet. When there is no mass there is no volume.

- When you have completed your graph, it should be similar to the one shown in Figure 1. Is it?
- Use your graph to predict the mass of exactly 4.0 cm^3 of copper. This process is called interpolation; it estimates an intermediate value between established data points on the graph.
- Use your graph to predict the mass of 9.0 cm^3 of copper. This process is called extrapolation because you have to extend the graph in order to estimate a value beyond the established range of the data.

Because the graph is a straight line you know that the ratio of the mass to the volume is a constant. In fact, the slope of the graph (the rise divided by the run), as shown in Figure 1, gives you the ratio.

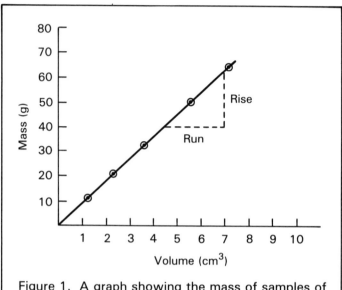

Figure 1. A graph showing the mass of samples of copper that have different volumes.

- What is the slope of the graph? (Don't forget the units!) What is another name for the slope of this graph?
- How can you use the slope to write an equation that will tell you the mass of any volume of copper? Use the letters M for mass and V for volume.

CURVED GRAPHS

The data in Table 2 show how the temperature of some hot water in a beaker changes with time.

Use the data in the table to make a graph in which you plot temperature on the vertical axis and time on the horizontal axis. (Notice that the vertical axis need only cover the temperature range from 55°C to 85°C.) Since the temperature readings were made at times that were determined by reading a clock, time is called the independent variable. Temperature is the dependent variable here

Table 2: The Temperature of a Beaker of Water as It Cools

Time (min)	Temperature (°C)
0	85.0
2	80.0
4	75.0
6	71.0
8	67.5
10	64.3
12	62.1
14	59.4
16	57.0

because its value depends on the time at which the thermometer was read. It is common procedure to plot the independent variable on the horizontal, or x, axis and the dependent variable on the vertical, or y, axis.

- What is the best way to connect the points you have plotted—with a curve or a series of straight lines from point to point?
- Once you have drawn the best graph you can for the data given, try to estimate the temperature of the water at 9 minutes. What is your estimate? What would you estimate the temperature to be at 20 minutes?

BIG NUMBERS AND SMALL NUMBERS

Materials needed: • knitting needles or thin sticks • index cards • marking pen • meter stick • long strip of paper, such as adding machine paper • tape • wrapping paper • 12 sticks, each 1 m long • clay

Before you prepare the next type of graph, which involves graphing data that extend over a wide range of numbers, you may find it useful to do this activity. It will help you develop a feeling for big (and little) numbers. Find a large area, such as an athletic field or a park. Since you will be placing markers along a number line, you will need a straight line on the field. This could be the sideline of a football or soccer field, a long string stretched across the length of the field, or the edge of the field itself.

Place a meter stick on the field next to one end of the line. Push a knitting needle, or a thin stick, into the ground at the zero end of the meter stick, which should be near the edge of the field. Make a big 0 (zero) on an index card and attach it to the needle or stick. Label additional knitting needles or thin sticks with cards that read 10^0 (1), 10^1 (10), 10^2(100), 10^3(1,000), as well as the following powers of 10: 10^4, 10^5, and 10^6.

- What numbers are represented by 10^4, 10^5, and 10^6?

    Use 1 millimeter (mm)—one-thousandth of a meter—as your unit length. Stick a second knitting needle, labeled 10^0, into the ground beside the 1 mm line on the meter stick. At the 10 mm, or 1 centimeter (cm), line, place the needle labeled 10^1.
- Where should you put the needle marked 10^2? 10^3? 10^4? 10^5?
- Stand back and look at what you have done. How does 10^2 compare with 10^1? That is, how many times bigger than 10^1 is 10^2? How does 10^3 compare with 10^1? How does 10^5 compare with 10^2? With 10^1?
- Can you place the needle labeled 10^6 on the field? Approximately where should it be placed?

    A hectare is an area equal to a square 100 m on a side. If the field is large enough, mark the corners of a hectare.
- How will you construct a right angle at each corner

of the square? (Hint: From the Pythagorean theorem, you know that a triangle whose sides are 3:4:5 is a right triangle.)
• How many square meters (squares 1 m on a side) are there in 1 hectare?

Any large number can be expressed as a small number times a power of 10. For example, the distance to the sun, which is 150,000,000 km, may be written 1.5 × 100,000,000 km, or, more easily, as 1.5×10^8. (Notice that the power to which 10 is raised equals the number of 0's following the 1.) When a number is written as a power of 10 multiplied by a coefficient between 1 and 10, it is called scientific notation.
• On the power of 10 scale you have laid out on the field, locate the following numbers: 150, 8.8×10^2, 86,000, 4.5×10^3, 2,500, 3.1×10^4.

To gain a feeling for small numbers, place a meter stick on a long strip of paper taped to a table or floor. Mark one end of the meter stick 0; mark the other end 1. This defines our unit length as 1 meter (m). Where is $\frac{1}{10}$, 0.1, or 10^{-1} on this new scale? Make a mark there and label it 10^{-1}. Find and label 10^{-2} (0.01 or $\frac{1}{100}$) and 10^{-3} (0.001 or $\frac{1}{1,000}$).

• Can you find and mark 10^{-4}? 10^{-5}? At what length, in meters, do you think something would be too small to be seen?
• How does 10^{-3} compare with 10^0? With 10^{-1}? With 10^2?
• Where are 0.82, 7.8×10^{-1}, 0.067, 5.6×10^{-2}, 0.006, and 4.5×10^{-3} on this scale?

Tape a large sheet of wrapping paper to the

floor. Draw a square 1 m on a side on the paper. The area within the square is 1 square meter ($1m^2$).
- How many square centimeters (squares 1 cm on a side) are there in 1 square meter? In 1 hectare?

Tape 12 meter sticks (or sticks that are 1 meter long) together to make a cube that is 1 meter long on every side. The space or volume inside this cube is 1 cubic meter ($1 m^3$).
- Use clay to make a cube that is 1 centimeter on each side. What do you think the volume of this cube is called?
- How many of the clay cubes would you need to fill a cubic meter? Express your answer in scientific notation.
- How many cubic millimeters (cubes 1 mm on a side) would have a volume equal to 1 cubic centimeter? How many cubic millimeters would you need to fill a cubic meter? To fill a cube with a base of 1 hectare and a height of 100 m? Express your answers in scientific notation.
- What is the volume of your room or classroom in cubic meters?

LOG GRAPHS

Sometimes it is not possible to fit all of the data on a uniformly divided axis because of the extraordinary range of the data. Here is an example. In the past 50 years information has emerged as one of the world's chief products. The principal factor behind this transformation has been the development of electronics technology, especially the integrated circuit, which is built on a single chip of silicon. These chips are the major components of the modern computer. Since the beginning of such circuitry in 1959, when one transistor fit on one chip, we have seen an incredible growth in the number of transistors that can be fabricated on a single chip. Table 3 shows this growth over a period of more than 30 years.

Obviously, the number of components cannot be plotted on a uniform numerical axis because the range—from 1 (10^0) to 100,000,000 (10^8)—can't fit on a sheet of graph paper. A convenient way to plot such a range of numbers is to use their exponents to make a graph.

Table 3: The Growth in the Number of Components per Silicon Chip

Year	Components per Chip
1959	10^0
1962	10^1
1965	10^2
1968	10^3
1972	10^4
1977	10^5
1982	10^6
1988	10^7
1992	10^8

The logarithm (log) of any number (in base 10) is the exponent to which 10 must be raised to equal that number. For example, the log of 1,000 is 3 because 10 must be raised to the exponent 3 in order to equal 1,000.

Make a graph of the exponents of the number of components per chip on the vertical axis and the year on the horizontal axis. It is important that the components axis be labeled "log components"; otherwise, someone reading the graph will not understand the wide range encompassed by the data.

Alternatively, you can label the components axis 10^0 (at the origin), 10^1, 10^2, and so on, at equally spaced intervals along the vertical axis.

- Did you notice that there are two distinct slopes to this graph? What happened to the rate of growth of components on a chip in about 1972?
- If, in 1970, you had tried to predict the number of components per chip that would be available in 1992, what would have been your answer?
- What is a necessary condition for using a graph to extrapolate?

Table 4: Logs Obtained with a Calculator

Number (N)	Number (N) as a Power of 10	Log of the Number (log N)
1,000	10^3	3.0
1,200	$10^{3.08}$	3.08
120	$10^{2.08}$	2.08
1.20	$10^{0.08}$	0.08
700,000	$10^{5.85}$	5.85
780,000	$10^{5.89}$	5.89
780	$10^{2.89}$	2.89
7,800	What is the answer?	?
4,620	What is the answer?	?

If the numbers we are dealing with are not as simple as in the previous example, you can use a calculator to find the log. For example, listed in Table 4 are a few logs that were found by using a calculator. Each log is the exponent to which 10 must be raised in order to obtain the given number.

Table 5 gives the density of the atmosphere (air) as a function of altitude. As you might expect, the density, measured in terms of the number of air molecules in each cubic meter of atmosphere, decreases as the altitude increases.

- Copy the table of data and add a third column to show the log of the air density.

Table 5: The Density of Air at Different Altitudes Above Sea Level

Air Density (Molecules/m^3)	Altitude (m)
$10^{17.4}$	100
$10^{16.1}$	200
$10^{15.3}$	300
$10^{14.6}$	400
$10^{14.0}$	500
$10^{13.5}$	600

- Make a graph of the log of the density versus altitude. Does it have a constant slope?
- Using the graph, what do you predict is the density of air at an altitude of 800 m?

Since $10^1 \times 10^2 = 10^3$, $10^3 \times 10^2 = 10^5$, and so on, it's evident that the product of two numbers can be obtained by adding their log values (exponents). A number written as $10^{2.5}$ might be written as $10^{0.5} \times 10^2$ or as 3.16×10^2 because $10^{0.5}$ is 3.16. Another way of saying this is that 0.5 is the log of 3.16.

- Write the air densities in Table 5 in scientific notation.

In Table 6, you'll find some data that pertain to the population growth of a colony of bees.

Table 6: Population Growth in a Bee Colony

Population	Time (days)
3,000	10
4,900	20
12,000	30
19,000	40
33,000	50

- Make a graph of bee population versus the time in days on regular graph paper. The population axis need only extend from 0 to 33 if you indicate that all population figures are multiplied by 10^3. You can do this by labeling the population axis "Bee population $\times$ 10^3."
- Predict the bee population after 45 days. After 55 days.
- Next, plot the same data using the log of the population figures. It is not necessary to find the values of these logs if you use semilog paper. Figure 2 shows a sheet of such graph paper. The horizontal axis is evenly spaced, but the vertical axis is not. The base line on the vertical axis is labeled one. It actually represents log 1, which is 0, since 10^0 is 1. The next numbered line, 2, is actually log 2 = 0.30. The line marked 3 is really log 3 = 0.48, and so on, up to log 10, which is 1. That covers the first cycle. The log of 20 is 1.30, which is the height of the first major division on the second cycle. The paper illustrated has two cycles. The second cycle can take us as high as 100. For numbers above 100 we need a third cycle. For numbers above 1,000 we need a fourth cycle.
- Make a graph of bee population for the indicated days using two-cycle semilog paper. Once again, you need only indicate that all populations are multiplied by 10^3.
- Predict the bee population after 45 days. After 55 days.
- Did the regular graph or the semilog graph give you more reliable predictions? Why?

PREDICTIONS FROM TABLES

To make reasonable predictions from tables of data it is often, but not always, necessary to make a graph of the

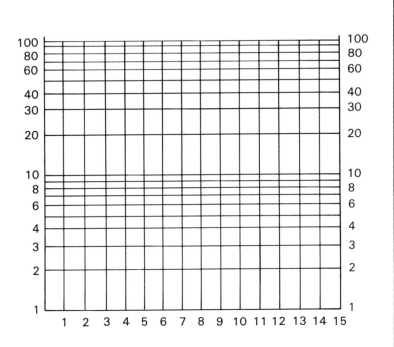

Figure 2. With semilog graph paper, you can plot the log of numbers without having to calculate the log. The spacings on the vertical axis represent logs to the base 10.

data. Table 7 gives some population figures for Japan and Nigeria.

- On the same axes, make a graph of population versus year for each country. Did the population of Nigeria ever equal that of Japan?
- Can you predict their populations in the year 2000? Compare the reliability of these two predictions. Which prediction do you feel is more realistic? Why?
- Compare the different curvatures of the two graphs. What does the curvature tell you about population growth in each country?

Table 7: Population of Japan and Nigeria from 1980 to 1990

Year	Japan Population (in Millions)	Nigeria Population (in Millions)
1980	116	74
1985	121	92
1990	124	119

HISTOGRAMS

Whenever we have a large sample of data that show the frequency of some particular observation or measurement, we can display the data with a histogram. The frequency is plotted on the vertical axis. The horizontal axis is divided into equal-width spaces, each representing a range of the value being measured or observed.

Suppose, for example, that a storekeeper records the number of customers entering a store each day. A record is kept for 45 days. The entries are as follows: 67, 44, 19, 45, 47, 74, 30, 60, 60, 32, 51, 49, 8, 59, 41, 32,

47, 68, 57, 43, 11, 68, 31, 48, 91, 52, 39, 15, 21, 40, 56, 41, 43, 21, 52, 27, 41, 28, 37, 39, 52, 35, 54, 55, 45.

Here are the same numbers reordered: 8, 11, 15, 19, 21, 21, 27, 28, 30, 31, 32, 32, 35, 37, 39, 40, 41, 41, 41, 43, 43, 44, 45, 45, 47, 47, 48, 49, 51, 52, 52, 52, 54, 55, 56, 57, 59, 60, 60, 67, 68, 68, 74, 91.

There are many ways that we can divide the horizontal axis. One way is to divide the number of customers into groups of 0–9, 10–19, 20–29, 30–39, . . . Figure 3 is a histogram of the data using such a division. It tells the storekeeper that usually 30 to 60 shoppers can be expected per day, but there will also be a few days when the store will be almost empty, and, more importantly, there will be times when 60 to 100 customers will have to be accommodated.

- Obtain the heights of all the players on a professional basketball team. Make a histogram of the data. Make a similar histogram for a professional baseball team. What do the histograms tell you?

SIGNIFICANT FIGURES

Materials needed: • ruler

In math and science, you are frequently asked to make measurements. If your measurements are to have meaning, they should be made and recorded in a careful and reasonable way. For example, it doesn't make sense to use a balance that is sensitive to 0.001 gram (g) if the larger masses used in making the measurement are off by 0.1 g. The ends of many rulers are rough and worn; consequently, it is better to start measuring an object at a clearly visible line further in on the ruler.

In making any measurement, you always have to estimate the final digit. For example, if you measure the length of a board with a ruler that has lines at 1-centimeter

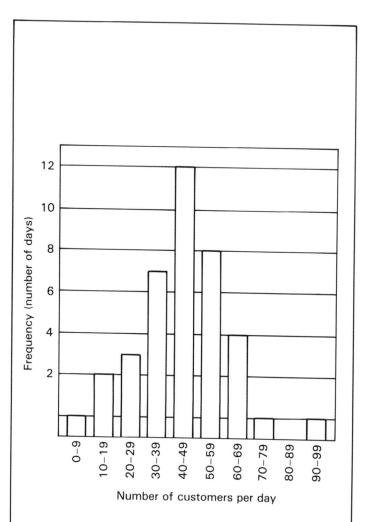

Figure 3. A histogram of the number of customers entering a store each day.

(cm) intervals, you will have to estimate tenths of centimeters in determining the length. If the ruler has lines at 1-millimeter (mm) intervals, you will be able to measure tenths of centimeters or millimeters, but you will have to estimate tenths of millimeters.

If you measure a metal cube and estimate one side of the cube to be 3.45 cm, you are certain that it is between 3.4 and 3.5 cm in length. You are less certain as to whether it could be 3.44 or 3.46, but you estimate it to be about halfway between the fourth and fifth millimeter lines following 3.0 cm. If you were to record the measurement as 3.456279 cm, the figures 6, 2, 7, and 9 would be meaningless; they would have no significance. Any number written after the 5 has no significance because you weren't even certain of the 5: you had to estimate it. In making any measurement, the first number that you have to estimate is the last significant figure in the measurement.

Using scientific notation in recording measurements will help you to express the proper number of significant figures. For example, if someone tells you a field is 1,200 m long, you can't be sure whether that measurement was made to the nearest 1 meter, the nearest 10 meters, or the nearest 100 meters. By writing the measurement as 1.200×10^3 m, the person who made the measurement tells you that he or she estimated the length to four significant figures, or in this case, to the nearest 1 meter. If the measurement had been measured to the nearest 100 m, it would have been recorded as 1.2×10^3 m.

- How would the measurement be recorded if it were made to the nearest 10 m? If it were made to the nearest decimeter (0.1 m)? To the nearest centimeter (0.01 m)?

Suppose you make careful measurements of the length and width of a metal cube and record them as 3.24×10^0 cm and 3.26×10^0 cm. Having measured the length and width to three significant figures, you decide to calculate the area of that side of the cube by using a pocket calculator to multiply the two numbers. You find the answer to be $10.5624\ cm^2$. But wait a minute! How can the product of two numbers that are only good to three significant figures produce a number that has six significant figures?

Of course, it's impossible. To see why, just remember that the third number in each of these measurements was estimated. Suppose both measurements were actually 0.01 cm too high or 0.01 cm too low, which is quite likely. In fact, they might be 0.02 or 0.03 cm too high or low.

- What is the product on your calculator if the numbers are actually 3.25 cm and 3.27 cm? If they are actually 3.23 cm and 3.25 cm?
- Compare these numbers with $10.5624\ cm^2$. What is the first digit, as you read from left to right, where the numbers do not agree? What was the first digit estimated in each measurement? How many significant figures were there in each measurement of length? How many significant figures are there in the calculation of the area?

A rule of thumb with regard to the multiplication and division of significant figures is this: The answer should have only as many significant digits as the measured number with the least number of significant digits.

- Suppose the height of the cube that was measured in the previous example is found to be 3.2 cm using a less accurate ruler. What is the volume of the cube? How many significant figures should there be in the answer?

Use a ruler to measure the length and width of a sheet of paper as accurately as possible. Then calculate the area.

- How many significant figures were there in each measurement? How many significant figures should be used in expressing the area? Would it make a difference if the area were expressed in square meters (m^2) rather than square centimeters (cm^2)?
- Show why the sum of 2.54 cm, 3.3 cm, and 6.187 cm should be 12.0 cm.
- Show why the difference between 12.9376 m and 1.9 m should be 11.0 m. Why should the difference between 12.9376 m and 10.9 m be 2.0 m?

SEARCHING FOR MATHEMATICAL PATTERNS IN SCIENCE

In Chapter 1 you learned some of the ways mathematics can be used in the never-ending search for patterns and relationships that characterizes science. In this chapter, you'll be using some of those mathematical methods in your own investigations. But we'll begin by examining a unique geometric pattern that appears to govern the growth of the chambered nautilus. It will help you to realize that patterns and relationships in nature often appear in unexpected places.

GEOMETRIC PATTERNS IN THE CHAMBERED NAUTILUS

Materials needed: • tracing paper • ruler • pencil

The chambered nautilus shown in the photograph is a beautiful example of the complex nature of living organisms. Even a superficial glance at the picture reveals that the nautilus grows by adding increasingly larger, but similar, segments to its body. But would you guess that in

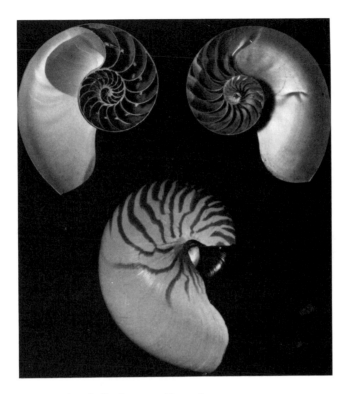

The shell of a nautilus, the sea creature shown at bottom, is split in two at top to reveal spiraling chambers. Can you see any pattern in the nautilus' growth?

doing so the nautilus follows a strict, but simple, geometric pattern?

Here is how you can discover the nature of this pattern for yourself. Figure 4 is an outline of the cross section of a nautilus. The base of a triangle, AB, can be drawn anywhere on the outline of the nautilus.

- Find the midpoint of AB and draw a perpendicular bisector on this base. The point where the perpendicular intersects the outline of the growing nautilus is labeled point C. Complete the triangle ABC. What do you notice about this triangle?

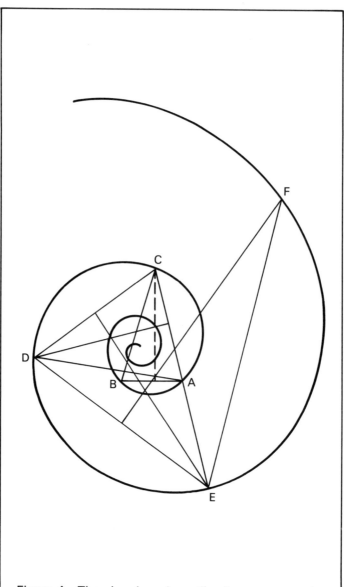

Figure 4. The chambered nautilus is programmed genetically to maintain beautiful symmetry as it grows.

Now repeat the procedure as outlined previously, using the line AC as the base of a new triangle. The point of intersection of the new perpendicular bisector and the outline of the growing nautilus is to be designated point D.

- What do you notice about triangle ACD?

Continue this procedure, constructing triangles CDE, DEF, and so on. Once the triangles have been drawn, find the ratio of the length of side CA to base AB. Continue finding the ratio of the similar side of each triangle to its base.

- How do these ratios compare?
- In your own words, what is the nautilus's geometrical growth plan?

REFLECTED LIGHT—A PATTERN OF ANGLES

Materials needed: • scissors • heavy black construction paper • dark room • lamp • plane mirror • small protractor • sheet of cardboard

Use scissors to cut a rectangle about 10 cm × 15 cm from a sheet of heavy black construction paper. Cut a narrow 1 mm-wide slit about 7 cm long in the center of the rectangle (see Figure 5). Fold the sides of the rectangle so the paper will stand upright on a piece of cardboard resting on a table. In a dark room, place a lamp bulb several meters from the table. Use the single bulb to illuminate the upright paper, which will serve as a "ray maker." Light passing through the slit in the paper will make a narrow beam that you can consider as a ray of light. Place the mirror along the edge of a small protractor. In that way you can measure the angle that the incoming (incident) ray of light makes with a perpendicular line (normal) to the mirror at the point where the ray hits the mirror. You can also measure the angle that the

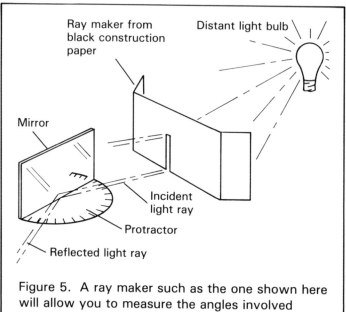

Figure 5. A ray maker such as the one shown here
will allow you to measure the angles involved
when light is reflected.

outgoing (reflected) ray makes with the same perpendicular. The angle between the incident ray and the normal
is called the angle of incidence. The angle between the
reflected ray and the normal is called the angle of reflection. How do the angles of incidence and reflection compare? Now turn the mirror and protractor to change the
angle of incidence. What happens to the angle of reflection? Repeat the experiment a number of times. In each
trial, change the angle of incidence until you have covered
a wide range of angles. Measure and record the angles
of incidence and reflection for every trial.

Make a table of your data. List the angles of incidence in one column and the corresponding angles of
reflection in a parallel column.

• How do the angles of incidence and reflection compare in each case you measured? Do you need to

make a graph to see the pattern in the data? If you do, plot the angle of incidence versus the angle of reflection. What pattern have you discovered?

FROM PATTERN TO PREDICTIONS
AND EXPLANATIONS

The discovery you made in the last section is part of the *law of reflection*. The second part of the law states that the rays of incidence and reflection lie in the same plane.

- How might you show that these rays do lie in the same plane?

The law of reflection, like all scientific laws, is a generalization based on a vast number of observations and experiments. Such laws enable us to make predictions and explain many common phenomena. For example, knowing the law of reflection you can predict the direction of the ray shown in Figure 6a after it strikes the mirror. By considering a second ray coming from the same point on the object, you can explain why all the points on a plane mirror image have corresponding points on the object. Of course, a mirror image arises because light rays coming from an object are reflected in such a way that they appear to be coming from behind the mirror. This can be seen in Figure 6b.

- From your knowledge of geometry (or by making scale drawings), the law of reflection, and the diagram in Figure 6b, show that the distance from the reflecting surface to the image behind the mirror equals the distance from the mirror to the object in front of the mirror.

The law of reflection is the basis for many innovations in engineering and technology. The periscope shown in Figure 7 is one example.

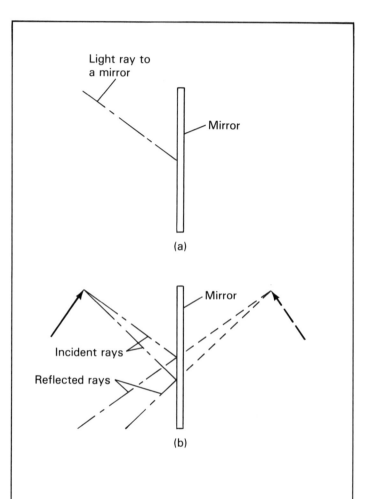

Light ray to
a mirror

Mirror

(a)

Mirror

Incident rays

Reflected rays

(b)

Figure 6. (a) Knowing the law of reflection, you can predict the direction the reflected ray will travel. (b) By considering two of the many rays from a point on an object (the tip of an arrow in this case), you can show that the distance from a point on an object to the mirror is half the distance from the point on the object to the corresponding point on the image behind the mirror.

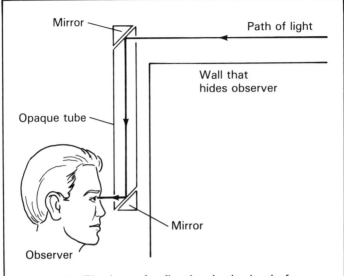

Figure 7. The law of reflection is the basis for many innovations in engineering and technology. The periscope is one example.

- How is the law of reflection used in building a periscope? What are some practical uses for periscopes?
- Design and build a periscope of your own. What materials will you need?

REFRACTED LIGHT—ANOTHER PATTERN

Materials needed: • pencil in glass of water • black construction paper "ray maker" used in previous section • clear, rectangular plastic box • water • dark room • lamp • small protractor • white paper • sheet of cardboard

When light passes through one transparent medium into another, it bends; we say the light is refracted. You can see this for yourself. Put a pencil in a glass of water.

Notice how the pencil appears to be bent or broken at the point where it enters the water. Light coming from the submerged part of the pencil is bent when it passes from water into air. Light that comes from the upper part of the pencil is not bent before it reaches your eyes because its path is through a single transparent medium— air.

To see more direct evidence of refraction, you can use the ray maker you used in the previous section to make a light ray that can pass from air into and out of a clear, rectangular water-filled box. The setup, which is shown in Figure 8, can be used in a dark room as before. A similar setup using a glass prism instead of water is shown in the photograph on the next page.

This straw appears to be bent because light reflecting from it underwater is refracted, or bent, when it passes into the air. What is the faint shape that slopes down to the lower right?

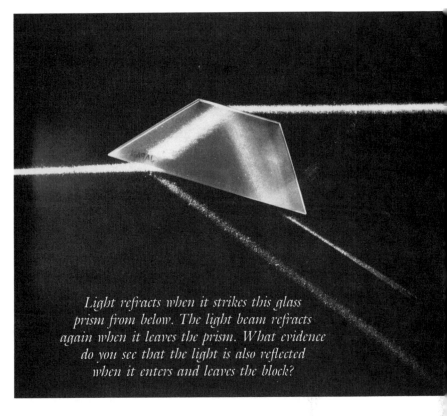

Light refracts when it strikes this glass prism from below. The light beam refracts again when it leaves the prism. What evidence do you see that the light is also reflected when it enters and leaves the block?

As you can see, light is bent when it enters and leaves water or glass. The photograph and your experiment show that light moves in a straight line from the point where it enters the water or glass to the point where it leaves. Bending occurs only at the points where it passes from one medium to another.

Just as before, when you investigated reflection, the angle of incidence is measured from a normal to the box at the point where the light ray enters the water. The angle between the normal and the refracted light ray in the water or glass is called the angle of refraction. From the photograph, you can see that some of the light is reflected when it strikes the glass. The rest of the light is refracted as it enters the glass.

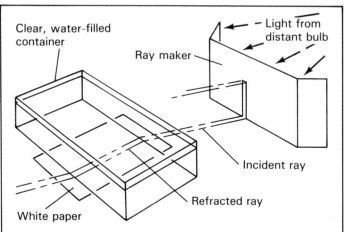

Figure 8. A ray maker can be used to make a light ray that will pass from air into and out of a clear, rectangular, water-filled box, as shown here. If the path of the light in the water is not clear, cut a piece of white file card to fit the bottom of the clear container.

In the figure, the following labels appear: Clear, water-filled container; Ray maker; Light from distant bulb; Incident ray; Refracted ray; White paper.

- How does the angle of refraction compare with the angle of incidence?

You could change the angle of incidence and measure the corresponding angle of refraction for a number of different angles. If you did, you would obtain data similar to those shown in Table 8 where the angles of incidence and the corresponding angles of refraction are given for light passing from air into water and from air into glass.

- For which angle of incidence is there no refraction (bending) of the light?

In this experiment we varied the angle of incidence from 0 to 80 degrees and measured the corresponding angles of refraction. The variable that we controlled—the angle of incidence in this experiment—is the independent vari-

Table 8: The Angles of Incidence and Refraction for Light Passing from Air into Water and from Air into Glass

Air into Water		Air into Glass	
Angle of Incidence (degrees)	Angle of Refraction (degrees)	Angle of Incidence (degrees)	Angle of Refraction (degrees)
0	0	0	0
20.0	15.0	20.0	13.1
30.0	22.1	30.0	19.5
40.0	29.0	40.0	25.5
50.0	35.0	50.0	31.0
60.0	40.5	60.0	35.4
70.0	45.0	70.0	38.8
80.0	48.0	80.0	41.0

able. The angle of refraction—the variable that we measured as we changed the independent variable—is the dependent variable. As you learned in Chapter 1, it is common practice to plot the independent variable on the horizontal axis and the dependent variable on the vertical axis. Thus, if we plot a graph of the angle of refraction as a function of the angle of incidence, the angles of incidence will be plotted on the horizontal axis and the corresponding angles of refraction on the vertical axis.

Using the data in Table 8, plot a graph of the angle of refraction as a function of the angle of incidence for light passing from air into water. On the same set of axes, plot a similar graph for glass using the data in the same table. The accuracy of the experimental values for water in Table 8 was about ±0.5 degree. That is, the experimenter was able to measure the angles to within about half a degree. Therefore, the points on the graph might be half a degree higher or lower on the vertical axis or half a degree to the right or left on the horizontal axis. You can indicate the range of error in your data by drawing a box around each data point.

- How large would each box be?
- Are the angles of incidence and refraction directly proportional for light passing from air to water? (If they are, the graph you have drawn will be a straight line that passes through the origin.) For light passing from air to glass?
- Do the angles of incidence and refraction appear to be directly proportional if you consider only small angles, say angles of incidence less than 40 degrees?

Using the data in Table 8, plot a graph of the sine of the angle of refraction as a function of the sine of the angle of incidence for light passing from air into water. The sine (sin) of an angle, θ, as shown in Figure 9, is defined as the ratio of y (the side opposite the angle) to r (the hypotenuse), that is,

$$\sin \theta = y/r.$$

Similarly, cosine (cos) $\theta = x/r$ and tangent (tan) $\theta = y/x$. (The sines of the angles in Table 8 may be obtained

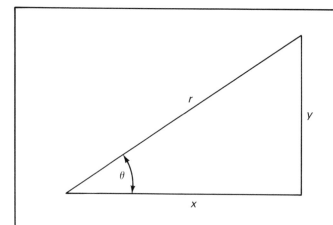

Figure 9. The sine (sin) of an angle θ is the ratio of y to r. The cosine (cos) of θ is x/r, and the tangent (tan) of θ is y/x.

by using a pocket calculator or from a mathematical table that gives the sines of angles from 0 to 90 degrees.)

- On the same set of axes, plot a similar graph for light passing from air into glass. Are the sines of the angles of incidence and refraction directly proportional for light passing from air to water? From air to glass?

EQUATIONS OF DIRECT PROPORTIONS

In Chapter 1, you found that plotting the masses of some pieces of copper as a function of their volumes produced a straight-line (linear) graph that passed through the origin. When the plotting of any two variables leads to such a graph, we say the variables are directly proportional. For any points on such a straight-line graph, the ratio of the two variables is the same.

$$\frac{y_1}{x_1} = \frac{y_2}{x_2} = \frac{y_3}{x_3} = \ldots$$

For any direct proportion, the relationship between the two variables can be expressed as

$$y \propto x,$$

where the symbol $\propto$ means "is proportional to." Such proportionalities can also be expressed as an equation of the form

$$y = mx$$

where m is a constant equal to the slope of the graph. That is,

$$m = \frac{y}{x}$$

for any corresponding values of y and x.

For the graph you drew in the previous section,

$$m = \frac{\sin r}{\sin i}$$

where r is the angle of refraction and i is the angle of incidence.

- What is the value of m for light passing from air to water? From air to glass?

By convention, the relationship between the angles of incidence and refraction is expressed as

$$n = \frac{\sin i}{\sin r}$$

where n is the index of refraction for the material in question.

- How are n and m related?
- What is the index of refraction for water according to your graph? For glass?

DISTANCE, SPEED, AND TIME

Materials needed: • long tube, or test tube, at least 15 cm (6 in) • rubber stopper or cap to seal tube or test tube • cooking oil • ruler • marking pen • stopwatch or watch or clock with sweep second hand or second mode • rubber bands • washers

Fill a long, clear tube or test tube nearly full with cooking oil. Leave enough space so that when the rubber stopper or cap is added, there will be a tiny air bubble in the tube. You will measure the speed of the air bubble as it moves along the tube.

- When the tube is level, the bubble remains at rest. What happens when you tilt the tube slightly?

You can determine how fast the bubble travels along the tube by measuring the time it takes the bubble to move a known distance. Dividing the distance by the time will give you the speed.

- If you tip the tube slightly and hold it steady, does the bubble appear to move at a constant speed?

To see whether the bubble really does move at a constant speed, use a marking pen and ruler to make evenly spaced marks along the tube as shown in Figure 10. Be sure to leave some space at the end of the tube to accommodate the stopper. In marking the tube, leave some distance at either end to allow for getting the bubble in motion before it reaches the starting line. If, after allowing for "bubble startup" at either end, you have 10 cm (4 in) of "track" available for the bubble, you could divide that length into four equal 2.5 cm (1 in) intervals. With a longer tube, you can have longer intervals or more intervals.

Once the tube is marked, fix it to the ruler with rubber bands. Then, if possible, ask someone to help you with this experiment. One person can watch the time

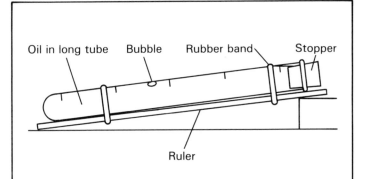

Oil in long tube   Bubble   Rubber band   Stopper

Ruler

Figure 10. To see whether a bubble moves at a constant speed in oil, time it using a watch or clock with a second hand and an oil-filled tube with evenly spaced marks.

while the other watches the bubble cross the lines on the tube. At a starting signal, lift one end of the ruler onto a small stack of washers. (In future runs, the ruler should always rest on the washers at the same point.) One person should call out, "Start!" at the moment the bubble's front end reaches the starting line. The other person should note the time (in seconds) or start the stopwatch at that moment. As the bubble moves along the tube, the time should be noted and recorded each time it reaches a line, including the finish line. It should take at least a minute for the bubble to travel along the "track."

Your data should give you a table of distances and times. Repeat the experiment several times to be sure the data are consistent.

Once you are satisfied that the data are reasonably consistent, plot a graph of the distance the bubble travels, in centimeters (or inches), as a function of the time, in seconds, required to travel that distance. Don't forget the point at the origin—in zero time the bubble travels zero distance.

- Is the graph close to being a straight line? Is the speed reasonably constant? How do you know?
- How can you use the slope of the graph to determine the bubble's speed? What is the speed in centimeters per second (cm/s) or inches per second (in/s)?

Now repeat the experiment, but make the angle between the tube and the table a little steeper. You can do this by adding washers to the stack on which the ruler rests.

Plot the data from this experiment on the same set of axes as before.

- Compare the two lines on the graph. How is the bubble's speed affected by the steepness of its path? How can you tell?
- Use the slope of the second line to find the bubble's new speed. What is it? How does it compare with the first speed?

You've seen that the slope of a distance versus time graph can be used to measure speed. Now use the speeds that you have determined from the graphs to plot graphs of speed versus time for the two experiments. (Use the same set of axes for both speed-time graphs.)

This may seem to be a trivial exercise to you because the speed is constant in both experiments; consequently, you'll obtain graphs that look like the one in Figure 11, where the speeds of two cars traveling at different constant velocities are plotted against time. Please bear with us because we're now going to ask you to find the area under the line in each graph you prepared. The results may surprise you. In the case of the graphs in Figure 11, the areas are 30 miles and 35 miles. Notice that when you multiply speed, which is distance per time, by time, the result is distance because the units for time cancel.

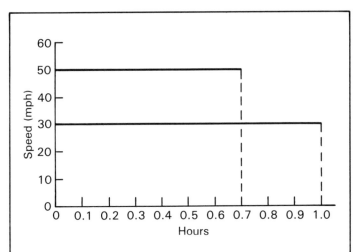

Figure 11. What is the area under each of these two graphs? One is for a car traveling 30 miles (48 km) per hour; the other for a car going 50 miles (80 km) per hour.

Therefore, the area under the line or curve in a speed versus time graph is the distance traveled. For example,

$$10\frac{m}{s} \times 10\text{ s} = 100\text{ m}$$

- What are the areas under the two lines in your speed versus time graphs? How do they compare with the distance the bubble traveled?

  Design and carry out an experiment to find out how the speed of the bubble in the tube you used is related to the angle of incline.
- Is it proportional to the angle? To the sine of the angle? To some other variable?

  Figure 12 shows the graph of speed versus time for a bicycle that starts from rest.
- What is happening to the bike's speed during the first 10 seconds? What information can you obtain from the slope of the graph during the first 10 sec-

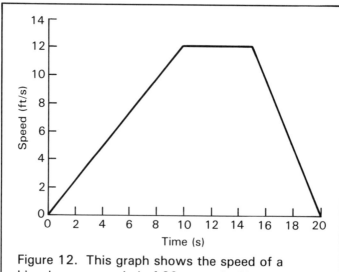

Figure 12. This graph shows the speed of a bicycle over a period of 20 seconds. How far did the bike go?

onds? How can you use the graph to determine how far the bike traveled during the first 10 seconds? During the interval from 10 to 15 seconds? From 15 to 20 seconds? What is happening to the bike during the last 5 seconds?

- Describe the trips shown by the velocity-time graphs in Figure 13*a* and the distance-time graphs in Figure 13*b*.
- Have a friend or classmate take a walk across a room. Can you sketch a distance versus time graph for his or her walk? (Just sketch it like the ones in Figure 13; don't try to use numbers.) Can he or she sketch a walk that you take across the room? Can you stump your graphing partner by walking faster and faster? By walking forward and then backward? By other walking strategies?
- Once you have sketched a number of distance versus time graphs for various walks, can you convert them to velocity versus time graphs?
- At another session, you might start by sketching velocity versus time graphs of the walks. Can you convert these graphs to sketches of distance versus time graphs?

PENDULUM PATTERNS

Materials needed: • string • tongue depressor • metal washers • paper clip • tape • stopwatch or clock or watch with second hand or second mode

Galileo realized that the to-and-fro motion of a pendulum could be used to keep time. But what factors control the rhythmic pattern of a pendulum clock? What makes it run fast or slow? And how can such a clock be adjusted to keep proper time?

Build a pendulum with string, a tongue depressor, a metal washer, a paper clip, and tape as shown in Figure 14. Ask an adult to make a slit in the tongue depressor

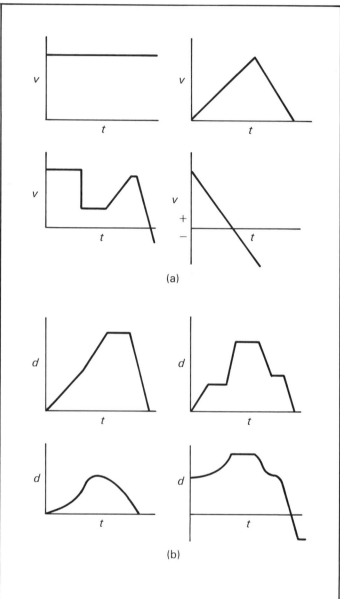

Figure 13. These sample graphs show (a) velocity versus time and (b) distance versus time.

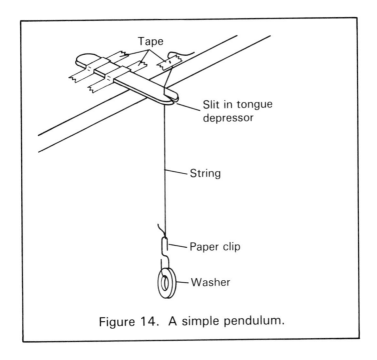

Figure 14. A simple pendulum.

with a sharp knife. The tongue depressor can be taped to the top of a door frame or some other high surface. You can change the mass of the bob by adding more washers to the paper clip. You can change the length of the pendulum, as measured from support point to center of bob, by changing the length of the string below the tongue depressor. The amplitude of the swing (its maximum movement) can be changed by pulling the bob farther to one side before releasing it.

To measure the period of a pendulum—the time for it to make one complete swing, over and back—count the number of swings in 30 seconds or 1 minute and then divide the time, in seconds, by the number of swings. Be sure to start timing when you release the bob. That moment is time zero *and* zero swings. Don't count "one" (1) until the pendulum has completed one complete swing (over and back).

Suppose the pendulum makes 40 complete swings in 30 seconds; the period of the pendulum then is

$$\frac{30 \text{ s}}{40} = 0.75 \text{ s}$$

To find out how the period of a pendulum is related to the amplitude of its movement, build a pendulum that is 1 meter long. Then pull the bob 2 cm to one side of its rest position and release it. Determine the pendulum's period and record it. Repeat the experiment, but this time pull the pendulum bob 4 cm to the side and release it. Again, determine the period and record it.

How does doubling the amplitude of the pendulum's swing affect the period? What can you say about the effect of the amplitude on the period?

To see how the mass of the bob affects the period, add a second washer to the paper clip. Check to be sure that the length is the same as it was before. Then pull the bob to one side and release it. Measure the period of the pendulum again.

- Why should the length be the same as before?
- Does it matter whether you pull the bob 2, 3, or 4 cm to the side before releasing it? Why?
- How does doubling the mass of the bob affect the period of the pendulum? What effect does the mass of the bob have on the period of a pendulum?

To see whether the length of the pendulum affects the period, lengthen the pendulum to 1.5 m and determine the period.

- What is the period of the pendulum now? How does lengthening the pendulum affect its period?

Predict what you think will happen to the period if the pendulum is shortened to 0.5 m. Test your prediction.

- Were you right?

To see whether there is a pattern—a mathematical relationship—between the period and the length of a pendulum, you'll have to measure the period for different lengths of the pendulum. Measure and record in a data table the period of the pendulum when its length is 0.10 m, 0.25 m, 0.5 m, 0.75 m, 1.0 m, 1.25 m, and 1.5 m. (You have already recorded some of these data.)

- Which is the independent variable, the length or the period?
- Can you tell from the data table whether or not the period is directly proportional to the length? If you can't, plot a graph of the period as a function of the length. (Don't forget the origin; if the length is zero, the period is zero.) What do you conclude?

Add a third column to your data table. In that column record the square of the period (period^2) for each of the periods you determined. Then make a graph of the period squared as a function of the pendulum's length.

- What do you conclude from the graph? Write the equation for the graph.

If this experiment were performed on the moon, your data table would look something like the one shown in Table 9.
Use these moon data to plot a graph of the period squared as a function of the length.

- How does this graph compare with yours? Write the equation for this "pendulum on the moon" graph.
- In addition to length, what other factor appears to affect the period of a pendulum?

Table 9: Hypothetical Measurements of the Period
of Pendulums on the Moon

Length (m)	Period (s)
0.10	1.6
0.25	2.5
0.50	3.5
0.75	4.3
1.00	4.9
1.25	5.5
1.50	6.0

A SPRING PENDULUM

Materials needed: • screen door or window shade spring • masses • stopwatch or watch or clock with sweep second hand or second mode

Hang a spring, such as a screen door spring or a spring from inside a window shade, from a support. Then hang a mass from the bottom of the spring. If you release the mass, you will see that it bounces up and down with a constant period.

- Is the period of this oscillating spring, like the period of a pendulum, independent of the mass that is hung on it?
- How is the period of the spring related to the mass that is attached to it?

FROM CURVED TO STRAIGHT-LINE GRAPHS

As you've seen, a graph that is a distinct curve can some-times be changed to a straight line by manipulating one of the variables. For example, you found that the period of a pendulum plotted as a function of its length was a curve. However, when you squared the period and plotted it as a function of the pendulum's length, the graph was linear. In fact, it showed that the period squared is directly proportional to the length.

- Would a plot of the pendulum's period as a function of the square root of the pendulum's length also produce a straight-line graph?

Now let's see how turning one variable upside down (inverting it) can sometimes produce a linear relationship. In Table 10, you'll find the density of a sample of air as its volume is decreased from 1.0 to 0.10 liter (L). This was done by compressing the gas in a closed container with a weighted piston.
- Why does the density of the gas increase as the volume decreases?

Plot a graph of the density of the air as a function of its volume.

- Is the density proportional to the volume? How can you tell?

Try plotting the density of the air versus the inverse of the volume (V), that is, versus $1/V$.

Table 10: The Density of a Sample of Air at 20°C as Its Volume Shrinks Because of Increasing Pressure

Volume (L)	Density (g/L)
1.00	1.18
0.80	1.48
0.60	1.97
0.40	2.95
0.20	5.90
0.10	11.80

- Is the density of the air proportional to the inverse of the volume? How can you tell? Can you write an equation for this graph?

When one variable is proportional to the inverse of another, we say they are inversely proportional. For example, the volume of a gas at a fixed temperature is inversely proportional to the total pressure on the gas. This relationship is known as Boyle's law because it was discovered by Robert Boyle, a seventeenth-century English scientist.

- For any inverse relationship, such as

$$Y \propto \frac{1}{Y} \text{ or } X = \frac{k}{Y}$$

what can you predict about the product of the two variables?

To test your prediction, copy the data in Table 10 and make a third column in which you write the product of the numbers in the first two columns.

- Do the numbers confirm your prediction?
- For the equation $X = k/Y$, how can you find the value of k? If X and Y are values obtained by measurement, how could you estimate the errors involved in making the measurements?

APPLYING MATHEMATICS IN DIVERSE WAYS

Mathematics is important in almost everything we do. In this chapter you will see how it is used in a few very different ways. You'll use mathematics in making estimates, which is something we all do every day whether we are aware of it or not. By using mathematics, you can make more reasonable and valuable estimates. In addition to making estimates, you'll see how mathematics is used in music, navigation, and even calculating how much of the food we buy is inedible.

THE ART OF MAKING REASONABLE ESTIMATES

Materials needed: • box of rice • balance or measuring cup • ruler • pencil • graduated cylinder • eyedropper • meter stick or yardstick • sheet of light cardboard • scissors

Finding exact numbers for most of the things we have to deal with is impossible. That is why newspapers, books, and conversations are filled with estimates—estimates of figures for the federal or state budget, of the costs involved in operating a school, of the number of people attending a parade, of the distance to a galaxy, of a country's population, of a molecule's size, and so on. From the very small to the very large, we are seldom able to determine the exact number of anything, but the art of making accurate estimates allows us to make reasonable decisions.

All of us make estimates every day of our lives. Most of them are made in response to simple, often subconscious questions: How long will it take me to do my homework? How much will the groceries cost? When should I apply the brakes to stop my bike at the intersection? Many are initiated in response to practical problems: How much paint will I have to buy to paint my house?

To answer the last question, you would first estimate the total area to be painted. Then you would find out how much area a gallon of paint covers. (It's printed on the can.)

- Suppose a gallon of paint will cover 30 square meters. What measurements would you want to make before you go to the store to purchase the paint?

When you go to your doctor for a physical examination, one of the things that is done in the tests that often follow or precede such an examination is a routine estimate of the number of red blood cells in each cubic millimeter of your blood.

If you have ever looked at your blood under a microscope, you know that it would be impossible to count all your red blood cells. Instead, a laboratory technician makes an estimate of the number of red blood cells in a small sample of your blood. He or she begins by drawing a tiny volume of your blood into a small pipette. One part of that blood is then diluted with 199 parts of a

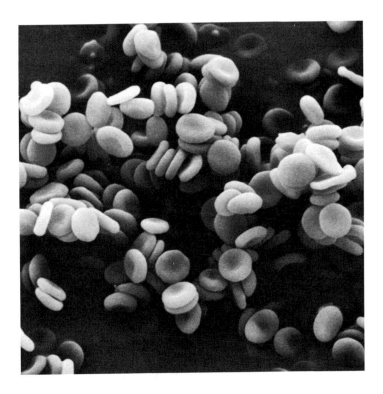

One cubic millimeter of blood contains millions of red blood cells like the ones seen here through a microscope.

saline solution, which gives a dilution of 1:200 (1 volume of blood in a total of 200 volumes of liquid). After mixing, a drop of your diluted blood is placed in a small counting chamber. The shallow chamber, which has a volume of 0.10 cubic millimeter, is divided by cross-rulings into 400 equal spaces. The volume of each space is, therefore, only $1/4,000$ mm^3.

The technician views the chamber through a microscope and counts the red blood cells in 80 of the 400 spaces. That number is then multiplied by 10,000 to find the number of cells per cubic millimeter. (The number counted is the number of cells in 1/50 (80/4,000) mm³ of solution. To find the number in 1 mm³, the technician has to multiply the number of cells by 50. Because blood makes up only 1/200 of the solution, the number must be multiplied again by 200 to find the number of red blood cells in 1 cubic millimeter. Since 50 × 200 is 10,000, the technician simply multiplies by 10,000 to find the number of cells per cubic millimeter.)

- The volume of blood in your body is about 4 to 5 liters. (One milliliter equals 1 cm³.) Estimate the total number of red blood cells in your body if the technician viewing your blood sample counts 500 cells in 80 squares.

The examples in the previous sections should give you some idea of what must be done to make reasonable estimates. Now, let mathematics and your common sense work together as you make some estimates of your own.

ESTIMATING GRAINS OF RICE

How many grains are there in a box of rice? To answer the question, you might begin by making an estimate. Of course, no one expects an exact number answer because it's very unlikely that two boxes contain the same number of grains anyway. But you can certainly make a reasonable estimate of the number. You will probably find a balance or a measuring cup useful in making your estimate.

- How many grains are there in a box of rice? Is it more or less than the number of red blood cells in a cubic millimeter of blood?

ESTIMATING BLADES OF GRASS

How many blades of grass are there on your lawn or a section of a park? Again, by counting the number of blades of grass in a small area you can estimate the number in a larger area that encompasses the lawn or park.

- How many blades do you estimate there are in the lawn or park?

ESTIMATING THE STARS VISIBLE IN THE SKY

You may have heard people say that they can see millions of stars in the sky. Do you think that's a reasonable estimate? You can find out by cutting a 10 cm × 10 cm square out of the center of a sheet of light cardboard. On a clear night, hold the square 30 cm from one eye and count the number of stars you can see within the square. Do this several times in different parts of the sky so that you obtain a reasonable average for the number of stars seen through the opening.

- What fraction of the sky's hemisphere do you see when you look through a 10 cm × 10 cm square held 30 cm from your eye?
- Estimate the number of visible stars in the sky. According to your estimate, about how many stars can be seen in the night sky?

OTHER ESTIMATES

Water has a density of 1.0 g/cm^3, and there are approximately 3.3×10^{22} molecules of water in 1 cubic centimeter.

- What is the approximate volume of a water molecule?
- What is your estimate of the number of molecules in a drop of water?

Here are some more estimates that you can do for practice. Do the ones that interest you most. If possible, ask some other people to make the same estimates so that you can compare results.

Estimate:
- The number of words in this book
- The number of books in your school's library
- The number of people at a football game or a parade
- The volume of soda consumed in the United States each year

Look for other things in your life where the art of estimating is useful.

- What are some of the estimates you make quite frequently?
- What are some estimates you would like to be able to make? Then see whether you can figure out how to make them.

MATHEMATICS AND MUSIC

If you pluck the string of a guitar, it vibrates at a constant frequency. The same thing happens when the hammer of a piano strikes one of the strings. The string vibrates a certain number of times each second. The rate of vibration—the frequency—depends on the tension, length, and material of the particular string. The string that is tuned to vibrate 440 times each second is called the A string. It produces the note we call A. This is true whether we are describing a guitar string or a piano string. Any instrument with a string vibrating at 440 vibrations per second is sounding the note A. (A frequency of 440 vibrations per second may be expressed as 440 hertz [Hz]—1 Hz is 1 vibration per second.)

What happens if we strike a key on the piano that vibrates at 880 Hz? To most ears, this note, when sounded with the 440 Hz string, gives a pleasing sensation. We say the notes are harmonious. Likewise, 220 Hz when sounded with 440 Hz is harmonious. It is customary to call 440 Hz *middle A*, 880 Hz *A above middle A*, and 220 Hz *A below middle A*. You can find harmonious notes on a stringed instrument by simply playing the whole string and then playing the same string at half its length.

The frequency interval between middle A (440 Hz) and A above middle A (880 Hz) can be divided in many ways. We could, for example, choose to divide this interval into seven equally spaced smaller intervals. Each tone, or note, would then vibrate at a fixed frequency. We call such a set of notes a scale.

What would such a scale sound like? Individually, each note of the scale would sound satisfactory to the ear. How would two notes, played together, sound? As we mentioned before, middle A when sounded with A above middle A would be harmonious. But it is not likely that most people would find pleasant harmony in any of the other combinations of notes. For this reason, no scale in which the 440 Hz between middle A and A above middle A is divided into seven equal intervals is used by musicians.

What then makes a scale harmonious? You can discover the answer to this question for yourself by analyzing a few scales that are commonly employed in music because they are so harmonious to our ears. In Western civilization the simplest scale is called the diatonic scale. It consists of eight familiar notes commonly called "do-re-mi-fa-sol-la-ti-do." Each note is labeled by a letter from A to G (and A again) and corresponds to a particular frequency or pitch. The higher "do" has twice the pitch (frequency) of the lower "do." But a scale can begin with "do" at any of the notes between A and G. For example, if we choose middle C, which has a frequency of 264 Hz, as "do," then to obtain harmony, we must divide the scale as shown in Table 11. This diatonic middle C scale is the C major scale, which is basic to most Western music. Eastern cultures find other scales more appealing.

- Find the *differences* in frequency between each of the successive notes in the C major scale; that is, subtract the frequency for C from the frequency for D, and so on. Are there equal frequency intervals between each pair of notes of the C major scale?
- Now find the *ratio* of each frequency to the frequency preceding it. For example, the ratio of the frequency of D to that of C is 297/264 = 1.125, or exactly 9/8. What are the remaining six ratios?

Table 11: The Diatonic C Major Scale

Vocal Note	Scale Note	Frequency (Hz)
do	C	264
re	D	297
mi	E	330
fa	F	352
sol	G	396
la	A	440
ti	B	495
do	C	528

Note: Only one octave—one set of eight notes—is included.

To find any pattern here we will need to look at another scale. In Table 12 you will find the diatonic scale of D Major. You may notice that some notes have slightly different frequencies than in the C major scale. Each note actually covers a small range of frequencies to which an instrument can be tuned.

Follow the same procedures as you did for the C major scale. That is, find the *differences* in frequency between each of the successive notes in the scale and the *ratio* of each frequency to the frequency preceding it. (These may not necessarily be exact fractions.)

Table 12: The Diatonic D Major Scale

Vocal Note	Scale Note	Frequency (Hz)
do	D	297
re	E	334
mi	F#	371
fa	G	396
sol	A	445
la	B	495
ti	C#	557
do	D	594

Note: Only one octave is included.

- Compare the results of the analyses of the two scales. What do you conclude?

To understand why F-sharp, F#, is so designated, notice that there is a frequency difference of $(396 - 352)$ Hz $= 44$ Hz between F and G. Adding half this difference, 22 Hz, to the frequency of F gives $(352 + 22)$ Hz $= 374$ Hz. This is just about the frequency designated for F#. We say that F has been raised a half-interval to F#. We can also say that G has been lowered a half-interval to G-flat, G♭. Similarly, C# or D♭ lies about halfway between C and D.

This is not the whole story by any means. A scale that includes all the sharps and flats is called a chromatic scale. One such scale is shown in Table 13.

- Repeat the same analysis for frequency differences and ratios that you followed for the diatonic scales.
- What determines the frequency intervals of the twelve tones of this chromatic scale?
- Why are there no E# or B# notes in the chromatic scale?

Table 13: The Equal Tempered Chromatic Scale

Scale Note	Frequency (Hz)
C	262
C#, Db	277
D	294
D#, Eb	311
E	330
F	349
F#, Gb	370
G	392
G#, Ab	415
A	440
A#, Bb	466
B	494
C	524

Note: *Only one octave is included.*

NAVIGATION, SAILING, AND MATHEMATICS

Materials needed: • ruler • protractor • map in Figure 15

There are no signs for travelers at sea or in the air above the earth as there are on highways. Consequently, navigators on ships, boats, and planes rely on the earth's magnetic field to plot their course from place to place. They determine the direction of the field from a compass. Unfortunately, the direction of the field varies from place to place depending on iron deposits and other materials found beneath the earth's surface. Thus, the compass needle often deflects to the east or west of true geographic north (the North Pole).

The circle and arrow near the bottom of the map in Figure 15 shows how far a compass needle deflects from true north at the coastal portion of New England shown in the map. There are places, such as parts of Florida, where this angle, known as the *magnetic declina-*

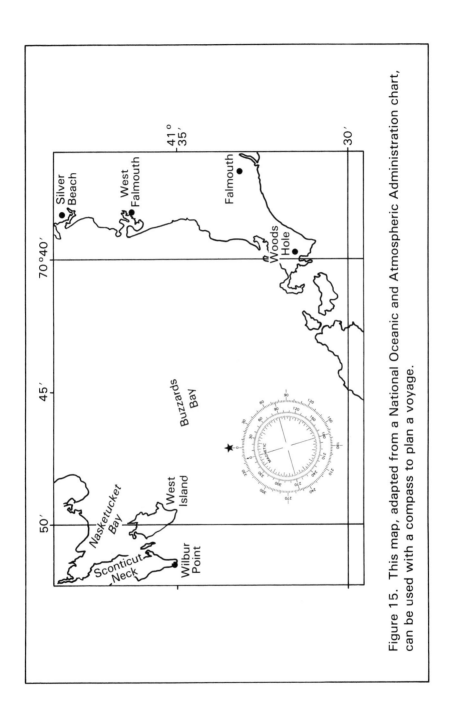

Figure 15. This map, adapted from a National Oceanic and Atmospheric Administration chart, can be used with a compass to plan a voyage.

tion, is zero. When connected on a map, these places form lines, called *isogonic lines*, along which a compass needle points toward true north.

Figure 15 is a portion of a chart supplied by the U.S. Dept. of Commerce National Oceanic and Atmospheric Administration (NOAA) for oceangoing vessels. NOAA charts give not only compass diagrams, but also the locations of shipwrecks, dump sites, soundings (depths of water), and bells. The compass diagram indicates true north by the star, and the geographic angles on the outer circle increase clockwise from the star. Inside these geographic markings are the angles marked "magnetic," which a magnetic compass would register when pointed in the direction of the corresponding geographic angle.

At the very center of the circle, you will find the magnetic declination, which sailors refer to as the *magnetic variation* (VAR). In Figure 15 the magnetic variation (declination) is 15° 00′ West. This tells us that at the location on a chart where this compass diagram is found, the magnetic compass points 15° west of true north. The date is also given because some magnetic declinations change with time. At this particular site, the words "no annual change" indicate the declination is constant throughout the year.

Imagine that it is a bright, sunny day and you are in a sailboat at latitude 41° 30.0′ N, longitude 70° 45.0′ W. Find your position on the chart in Figure 15. You want to sail to Wilbur Point at the southern end of Sconticut Neck on the other side of Buzzards Bay. You know that the distance from your position to the southern tip of West Island is 6.0 nautical miles.

- In what direction (angle) should you sail with respect to true (geographic) north?
- Since it is nighttime, you must rely on the boat's compass to determine direction. In what direction should you sail according to your compass?

*If you were sailing this boat in Buzzards Bay
off the coast of Massachusetts, could you
use a compass to determine the direction
you should sail to get to Wilbur Point?*

- If you can sail in a reasonably straight line at a speed
  of 5 knots (5 nautical miles per hour), how long
  will it take you to reach Wilbur Point?
- A nautical mile is 1.15 miles. What is the speed of
  your boat in miles per hour?

MATHEMATICS AND FOOD

Materials needed: • orange • tape measure

Many of the fruits and vegetables we eat are peeled; others have a pit or core that is discarded. What fraction of the food we buy do we eat and what portion do we throw away? Applied mathematics can provide an answer.

Consider an orange. Since it is very nearly a sphere, you can assume its volume is 4/3 πr^3, where r is the radius of the orange. To find the diameter of an orange, wrap a measuring tape around its "equator" to get its circumference, C. Since

$$C = \pi d = 2\pi r,$$

you can easily calculate the diameter and radius of the orange.

- How can you find the volume of the orange once you know its diameter?
    Now peel off the orange's thick skin, and using the same procedure as before, determine the diameter of the peeled orange.
- With this information, you can calculate the volume of the edible part of the orange. What is it?
- How can you calculate the volume of the orange's skin (which you may assume has a uniform thickness)? What is it?
- How can you use the information you have gathered and your calculations to calculate the thickness of the orange peel? (Remember, the surface area of a sphere is 4 πr^2.) According to your calculations, what is the thickness of the orange peel?
- Measure, as accurately as you can, the thickness of the skin directly. How do the two determinations of the thickness compare?
- What fraction of an orange is edible?
- Design methods to find the edible fractions of a banana, a peach, a plum, an apple, and a melon.

4

SPORTS AND MATHEMATICS

Sports analysts, announcers, statisticians, coaches, and athletes all make use of science and mathematics in their work. In this chapter, mathematics will help you answer such questions as: How fast do record-holding athletes run, swim, or round the bases? How are the rates of improvement in certain athletic events changing with time? Do athletes run faster indoors than they do outdoors? Do left-handed athletes have an advantage in baseball? How much does a baseball curve? What makes a ball follow a curved path?

MEN'S FREESTYLE SWIMMING: WORLD RECORDS

Table 14 contains some world records for men's freestyle swimming. By plotting graphs from the data in this table, you can make some predictions for events that are not listed.

- Draw a distance versus time graph using the data in Table 14. Does the graph help you to see what

United States Olympic swimmer Debbie Babashoff swims in a freestyle race. How fast can a good freestyle swimmer move through the water? Why do swimmers move more slowly than runners?

Table 14: Some World Records for Men's Freestyle Swimming

Distance	Time	Holder	Country	Date
100 m	0 min 48.42 s	M. Biondi	U.S.A.	1988
200 m	1 min 46.69 s	G. Lamberti	Italy	1989
400 m	3 min 45.00 s	E. Sadovyi	Unified Team	1992
800 m	7 min 47.85 s	K. Perkins	Australia	1991

happens to a swimmer's average speed as the length of the race increases?

- Kieren Perkins also holds the world record for the 1,500-m freestyle. What do you predict was his time in this race? How did you make your prediction?

- What do you predict is the record time in the 50-m freestyle? How did you make your prediction?
- To verify these predictions, find the average speed for each race. Then make a graph of average speed versus distance.
- Now predict the average speed for the 50-m race and use this value to find the time. Do the same for the 1,500-m race.
- Which of your two methods of predicting do you think is likely to be more accurate? Why?

SPEED AND DISTANCE

From what you learned about swimmers' speeds, you might guess that a runner's speed in a track event is related to the distance that he or she must run. You can check your guess by using the data supplied in Table 15, which shows the record times for a number of indoor track events.

Determine the average speed, in meters per second (m/s), for the runners in each event. Then plot a graph of speed versus distance for the men and for the women. Both graphs can be plotted on the same set of axes.

- How do the average speeds of the male and female runners compare?
- If B. Johnson and A. Issajenko had run in the same 200-m event, about how far apart would they have been at the finish line?
- In general, how does the speed of the runners change as the distance of the event increases?
- How can you explain the *increase* in average speed as the event distance increases from 50 m to 200 m?
- Use the graphs you have drawn to predict the speed of recordholders in the 100-m indoor event.
- Estimate the average speed of freestyle swimming and speed skating recordholders in their respective

Table 15: World Track and Field Indoor Records (as of February 1992) for Men and Women

Men			Women		
Event Distance	Record Time	Record Holder	Event Distance	Record Time	Record Holder
50 m	5.55 s	B. Johnson	50 m	6.06 s	A. Issajenko
60 m	6.41 s	Andre Cason	60 m	6.96 s	Merlene Ottey
200 m	20.36 s	B. Marie-Rose	200 m	22.24 s	Merlene Ottey
400 m	45.02 s	Danny Everett	400 m	49.59 s	J. Kratochvilova
800 m	104.84 s	Paul Ereng	800 m	116.40 s	C. Wachtel
1,000 m	135.26 s	N. Morceli	1,000 m	154.80 s	B. Kraus
1,500 m	214.16 s	N. Morceli	1,500 m	240.27 s	Doina Melinte
3,000 m	456.36 s	E. Puttemans	3,000 m	513.82 s	Elly Ven Hulst
5,000 m	800.40 s	S. Nyambui	5,000 m	903.17 s	Liz McColgan

500-m and 1,500-m events. Then check your estimates by consulting an almanac or another reference book. How good were your estimates?

- There are claims that some professional hockey players can skate at speeds of 30 mph (13.4 m/s). On the basis of your determination of the velocities attained by speed skaters, do these claims seem reasonable?

SPLIT TIMES FOR A RECORD-SETTING RUN

You may still be pondering why the average speed for the 200-m dash is greater than the average speed for the 50-m or 60-m dash. If that is the case, the data in Table 16 may help you to understand the reason. The table shows the split times for Carl Lewis's record-setting 100-m run at the World Track and Field Championships held in Tokyo in August 1991.

How fast can a good sprinter like Carl Lewis run? Is his speed constant throughout the race?

Table 16: The Measured Times over 10- or 20-Meter Intervals in Carl Lewis's Record-Setting 100-Meter Run

Distance Interval (m)	Time to Run Interval (s)	Total Time (s)
0–10	1.88	1.88
10–20	1.08	2.96
20–30	0.92	3.88
30–40	0.89	4.77
40–50	0.84	5.61
50–60	0.84	6.45
60–70	0.84	7.29
70–80	0.83	8.12
80–100	1.74	9.86

- What was Lewis's average speed for this 100-m run?
- During which 10-m or 20-m interval of distance did he run with the greatest average speed? What was his speed over this interval?
- During which 10-m or 20-m interval of distance did he run with the least average speed? What was his average speed over this interval?
- Use the data in Table 16 to plot a graph of distance as a function of time. Connect the points in the most reasonable way you can. How can you use the slope of the graph to determine the times when Lewis was running slowest? Fastest?
- Over what distance intervals was he running at a fairly constant speed? What was that speed? If he had run the entire race at this speed, how long would it have taken him to run the 100-m distance?
- Acceleration is the rate at which speed changes with respect to time. How can you use the graph to find the time interval during which Lewis's acceleration was greatest? Does the graph show any evidence of a deceleration (a decrease in speed over time) at any time during the run?
- Calculate the average speeds for each distance interval in the table and use those values to plot a bar graph of speed as a function of time. How can you use this graph to determine when Lewis's acceleration was greatest? (Remember, his initial speed was zero.) Does your determination of the time of his greatest acceleration on this graph agree with what you found using the distance versus time graph? Does this graph show any deceleration?
- How can you use this velocity-time graph to determine the distance that Lewis traveled during the run? If you determine the distance, how closely does it agree with the known distance of 100 m?
- Having examined Lewis's split times for a record-setting run, can you explain why the average speed

for the record-setting 200-m run is greater than the average speed for the record-setting 50-m dash? Do you think this will always be true? Why?

INDOOR AND OUTDOOR TRACK

Compare the record times for various indoor and outdoor track events. You can find this information in an almanac or another reference book at your school or local library.

- Do people seem to run faster indoors or outdoors? Why do you think this is?
- Compare the average speeds of recordholders for indoor and outdoor events of various distances from 100 m to 5,000 m. Does the ratio of the indoor to the outdoor speed for these events seem to remain constant or does it change with the distance of the race? How can you explain this?

EVER-IMPROVING ATHLETES, THE OLYMPIC 100-METER RUN, AND MORE

The modern Olympic Games owe their origin to the ancient Greek Olympic Games that were first held in Olympia in 776 B.C. The modern games began in 1896 with nine nations participating and have grown to include most of the world's countries today. (There were no Olympic Games in 1916, 1940, and 1944 because of World Wars I and II.)

A review of the winning times, distances, heights, and so on, in Olympic events reveals that athletes have improved dramatically during the past century. For example, prior to 1954 many people thought the mile would never be run in less than 4 minutes. They believed it would require a speed that exceeded the capacity of any human being. But in 1954 Roger Bannister ran a mile in 3 minutes, 59.4 seconds. Today, it is not unusual to see a race in which all the competitors run the mile in less than 4 minutes.

Many current athletes, bursting with confidence as new records are established every year, claim there are no limits to the speeds, distances, lengths, and heights that athletes can run, throw, and jump. Do you agree?

We'll begin by looking at the Olympic records for the 100-m dash since 1896. The 100-m dash is a very special test of a runner's skill because it's all over in about 10 seconds! There is an initial felinelike burst of energy that propels the runner forward from the starting line; then there are a few seconds of sustained speed before the final incredible surge to reach the finish line.

Table 17 lists the winning times for the Olympic 100-m run for both men and women since 1896.

On the same set of axes draw two graphs of winning time versus year—one for the men and one for the women.

- How do the rates at which the men and women are lowering their record times compare?
- According to the graph, in what year will women run the 100-m race in the same time as men?
- Can you predict whether, in the future, women will be running this race faster than men?

You might enjoy making similar investigations for other Olympic events. In an almanac or reference book you can find the winning times for various Olympic events—in some cases the records may go as far back as 1896. To see how athletes have improved over the past four to five decades, you can make a chart of the winning times for the Olympic Games champions in the 200-m, 400-m, 800-m, and 1,500-m runs. Collect the records of these events for both men and women. Then plot a graph of winning speeds versus Olympic year from as far back as you can find data to the present. Do this for each event for both men and women. By using different colored

Table 17: Winners of the Olympic 100-Meter Run, 1896–1992

Year	Runner (Men)	Time (s)	Runner (Women)	Time (s)
1896	Tom Burke, U.S.A.	12		
1900	Francis Jarvis, U.S.A.	11.0		
1904	Archie Hahn, U.S.A.	11		
1908	R. Walker, S. Africa	10.8		
1912	Ralph Craig, U.S.A.	10.8		
1920	C. Paddock, U.S.A.	10.8		
1924	H. Abrahams, G. Britain	10.6		
1928	P. Williams, Canada	10.8	E. Robinson, U.S.A.	12.2
1932	Eddie Tolan, U.S.A.	10.3	M. Jackson, Australia	11.9
1936	Jesse Owens, U.S.A.	10.3	H. Stephens, U.S.A.	11.5
1948	Hamson Dillard, U.S.A.	10.3	F. Blankers-Koen, Neth.	11.9
1952	L. Remigino, U.S.A.	10.4	M. Jackson, Australia	11.5
1956	Bobby Morrow, U.S.A.	10.5	B. Cuthbert, Australia	11.5
1960	Armin Hary, Germany	10.2	Wilma Rudolph, U.S.A.	11.0
1964	Bob Hayes, U.S.A.	10.0	Wyomia Tyus, U.S.A.	11.4
1968	Jim Hynes, U.S.A.	9.95	Wyomia Tyus, U.S.A.	11.0
1972	Valery Borzov, USSR	10.14	R. Stecher, E. Germany	11.07
1976	H. Crawford, Trinidad	10.06	A. Richter, W. Germany	11.08
1980	Allen Wells, G. Britain	10.25	L. Kongratyeva, USSR	11.6
1984	Carl Lewis, U.S.A.	9.99	E. Ashford, U.S.A.	10.97
1988	Carl Lewis, U.S.A.	9.92	F. Griffith-Joyner, U.S.A.	10.54
1992	L. Christie, G. Britain	9.96	Gail Devers, U.S.A.	10.82

pens or pencils to distinguish events and men from women, you can plot all your data on the same set of axes.

- Is there any evidence that women athletes are improving at a faster rate than men in any of these events? If so, what is the evidence and how is it revealed in the graphs you have drawn?
- Do any of today's women athletes run faster than men did in 1948? If you can find the records, do any of today's women athletes run faster than male athletes did in 1920?

- If you extrapolate your graphs, when might you expect women athletes to be running as fast as men in these events? Do you think it is reasonable to make such extrapolations? Why or why not?

In the same almanac or reference book, you can probably find the winning times, distances, lengths, or heights for a number of other Olympic events such as the marathon, hurdles, relays, discus, shot put, javelin and hammer throws, long jumps, high jumps, and various swimming events. You can prepare similar graphs for these events for both men and women.

- How does the improvement rate for men and women compare in these events?
- In which event or events does there seem to have been the greatest change in winning time, distance, length, or height? In which event or events does there seem to have been the least change?
- Can you explain the variation in the rate of improvement in speeds, distances, lengths, and heights for different events? In the pole vault, for example, can you see the effect of the more flexible fiberglass poles introduced in the early 1960s?
- If you extrapolate the graphs, do any of them seem to indicate a limiting barrier? Do any of the graphs reveal what might have been considered a barrier in an earlier decade that has since been broken? If so, what might explain the change in attitude?

BASEBALL AND SOME STATISTICS

The ratio of right-handed to left-handed people in the general population is 9 to 1. If you're a baseball fan, you know that despite the large number of people who play baseball, one in every nine catchers is not left-handed. In fact, there are *no* left-handed catchers, second basemen,

Cincinnati Reds catcher Johnny Bench throws to second base. Why are there no left-handed catchers in the major leagues?

third basemen, or shortstops in the major leagues. That's a simple, straightforward statistic. On the other hand, left-handed first basemen are considered to have an advantage over right-handers playing the same position.

• Why are the only left-handed major league infielders found on the pitching mound or at first base?

Consult a baseball encyclopedia and an almanac or a book of facts in order to make a list of the winners of batting championships in the two major leagues over a period of 25 to 30 years or more.

- Over these years, how many batting championships were won by left-handed hitters? By right-handed hitters? How does the ratio of right-handed to left-handed batting champions compare with the ratio of right-handed to left-handed people in the general population? What factors might explain this batting championship statistic?
- What is the ratio of right-handed to left-handed batters in the major leagues? Of right-handed to left-handed pitchers? How do these ratios compare with the 9:1 ratio among the general population?
- What additional data might you collect to see whether the ratio of right-handed to left-handed players found in baseball is justified?

SPEED ON THE BASE PATHS

Materials needed: • fast-running baseball player • baseball field with dirt (not grass-covered) base paths • stopwatch • long tape measure

Ask a baseball player who has good speed on the base paths to help you with this experiment. First, ask the player to run 110 meters (360 feet) along a straight-line path, while you time the run with a stopwatch.

- What was the player's average speed for this straight-line dash?

  After you have raked the base paths so the player's tracks will be easily seen in the dirt, ask the player to make a second run. This time ask him or her to run the same distance (110 m) around the bases (from home plate to first, to second, to third, and back to home), while you again measure the time with a stopwatch.

- What was the player's time for this run? How does it compare with the time along a straight path?
- Assuming the player ran 110 m in running the base paths, what was his or her average speed around the bases?

   To determine the player's true average speed in rounding the bases, you can use a tape measure to find the actual distance the player ran. The player's footprints will allow you to locate the path he or she followed in going around the base paths.
- What was the actual distance the player ran while circling the bases?
- What was the player's true average speed in going around the bases? Was it less than, more than, or the same as the player's average speed along a straight-line path?
- You have taken the actual distance of the run around the bases into account in calculating the true average speed. What other factors might have led to the change in the player's average speed?

CURVE BALLS

Materials needed: • Styrofoam ball or beach ball • baseball (optional) • tennis ball and racket (optional) • basketball (optional)

If you don't believe pitchers can actually make a ball curve, try this. Hold a Styrofoam ball or a beach ball in both hands. As you push the ball forward with one hand, use the other hand to give the ball a spin about a vertical axis as it leaves your hands. Watch the ball closely after you release it.

- Of course, the ball follows a curved path as it falls because of gravity, but does it also curve to the right or left?

Repeat the experiment a number of times. Watch what happens when you give the ball a clockwise spin (seen from above) and when you give it a counterclockwise spin. If you play baseball, perhaps you can make a baseball curve by turning your wrist as you release the ball.

If you play tennis, see whether you can curve your serve by applying spin to the ball when you hit it with the racket. If you play basketball, see whether you can make a bounce pass move right or left after the bounce by putting English (a spin) on the ball when you release it.

- Does the direction that the ball curves (to the right or left) depend on the direction of the spin that you give the ball when you release it? Can you formulate a rule that will allow someone to predict the direction that a ball will curve on the basis of the direction of its spin as it moves in a particular direction through air?

In carefully performed experiments, a baseball was dropped through a height of 6 feet in a wind tunnel. Before it fell, the ball was set into rotation by a machine. As it fell, air moved by the ball at controlled speeds to simulate the rate at which air might move by a ball thrown horizontally by a pitcher. When the ball was released without spin, it was blown slightly backward by the wind, but it was not deflected to the right or left. If the ball was spinning when released, it was deflected to the right or left as it fell. The deflections, which were originally measured in inches, are reported in units of both inches and meters in Table 18. Similarly, the wind speed is given in feet per second, meters per second, and miles per hour.

- Perhaps the deflection of the ball is proportional to its rate of spin. To find out whether it is, you must

Table 18: The Lateral Deflection of a Spinning Baseball During a 6-Foot Drop Across a Wind Tunnel

Ball's Rate of Spin (rev/s)	Wind Speed (ft/s)	(m/s)	(mph)	Deflection (in)	(m)
20	75	22.9	51	6.1	0.15
20	100	30.5	68	11.7	0.297
20	125	38.1	85	17.8	0.452
20	150	45.7	102	26.0	0.660
30	75	22.9	51	9.4	0.239
30	100	30.5	68	17.5	0.445
30	125	38.1	85	25.8	0.655

Source: Lyman J. Briggs, American Journal of Physics 27 (1959): p. 591.

consider tests at the same wind speed; otherwise, there would be no way of telling whether the deflection was due to the rate of spin or the wind speed. Notice that the table provides two different rates of spin at several different wind speeds. How can you use the data in the table to determine whether the deflection is proportional to the ball's rate of spin? What do you find?

- To see whether there is a relationship between the deflection of the ball and the rate at which air moves by the ball, you must compare data taken at the same spin rate. Why?

Choose a fixed rate of spin, say 20 rev/s, and plot a graph of deflection versus wind speed. (Don't forget to plot the origin—zero deflection for zero spin.)
- Is the graph a straight line? What does this tell you?

Next, try a graph of deflection versus the square of the wind speed.

- What do you find? What does this graph tell you? What is the relationship between the deflection of the ball and the speed of the air moving by it?
- Pitchers claim that in throwing a curve ball from the pitcher's mound to home plate, the ball's deflection can be increased by giving it more spin. However, they maintain that the ball's deflection is about the same whether they throw the ball at 60 or 90 mph. Does a ball, given a fixed rate of spin, curve by the same amount between the pitcher's mound and home plate regardless of its speed? Hint: Consider the number of turns the ball will make in its journey from the pitcher's mound to home plate, which is 60.5 ft (18.4 m) away.

ELECTRICITY, HEAT, AND MATHEMATICS

It would require several books to cite the many uses of mathematics in electricity and heat. Consequently, in this chapter you'll apply mathematics to only a few of the ways it can be used in these areas of science. You'll begin by investigating how to use mathematics in choosing the most economical electric light bulb to buy. Then you'll see how an early scientist arrived at a law that governs the relationship between electric current and voltage for a simple circuit involving a battery and a wire. By experiment, you will find the amount of heat required to raise the temperature of 1 g of washers through 1 degree Celsius (1°C). Finally, you will investigate the simple mathematical pattern materials exhibit as they expand when heated.

CHOOSING THE "BEST BUY" LIGHT BULB

Faced with a choice in buying a light bulb, you have a lot to think about if you want the "best buy." Common incandescent bulbs have a wide variety of wattages. Some are "regular;" some are "long-life." There are also fluorescent bulbs and halogen bulbs, both in a wide variety of specifications. Recently, a new bulb that uses a high-frequency radio signal instead of a filament has been introduced. It is called an "E lamp." How does one go about choosing the best bulb to buy?

Let's begin by considering only regular incandescent bulbs. You can find a wide variety of such bulbs at a supermarket or a hardware store. Each bulb will have a number of specifications on its package. Make a data table of the specifications for as many different bulbs as you can find. The table should include the bulb's wattage, average life, lumens, and cost.

The best buy, in the case of a light bulb, is the bulb that provides the most light energy for the dollar. The bulb's wattage is the amount of energy required per unit time to operate the bulb. A larger unit of energy per time is the kilowatt (kW). There are 1,000 watts (W) in a kilowatt (kW); therefore, a 100-W bulb is the same as a 0.100-kW bulb.

To find the amount of electrical energy required to operate a bulb, you can multiply the wattage, which measures the energy used per time, by the time the bulb is used:

$$\frac{energy}{time} \times time = energy.$$

The energy required to operate a 100-W bulb for 1 hour is

$$0.100 \text{ kW} \times 1 \text{ h} = 0.100 \text{ kilowatt hour, or } 0.100 \text{ kWh.}$$

(We will use kilowatt hours to measure energy because electric-power companies use that unit.)

- Ask a parent whether you may see last month's bill from your electric-power company. For how much electrical energy were you charged last month? What was the average cost in cents or dollars per kilowatt hour?

To find the best buy bulb, you need to know the amount of light energy delivered by each bulb over its lifetime. The sum of the cost of that energy and the cost of the bulb, when divided by the total cost of operating the bulb, will allow you to compare bulbs and thus find the best buy.

The usable wattage of the bulb, that is, the light energy emitted by the bulb per time, is not the same as the wattage marked on the bulb. Only a small fraction of the energy fed into the bulb produces light. Much of the electrical energy that enters the bulb is changed to heat, and much of the radiant energy produced is not visible light. The usable energy (light) emitted is indicated on the bulb specifications as "lumens." A lumen is simply a unit of luminous wattage. There are 683 lumens in a watt, so you can convert a bulb's lumens to watts by dividing the number of lumens by 683. For example, a 100-W bulb that delivers 1,710 lumens of usable light delivers

$$\frac{1,710 \text{ lumens}}{683 \text{ lumens/watt}} = 2.50 \text{ W}$$

(Notice that the usable wattage—the power that appears as light—is only 2.5 percent of the input.)

The total energy, in kilowatt hours, to operate a bulb over its lifetime is given by

$$\text{bulb wattage} \times \frac{1}{1,000} \times \text{average life (hours)}.$$

For example, a 100 W bulb with an average life of 750 hours uses

$$100 \text{ W} \times \frac{1 \text{ kW}}{1,000 \text{ W}} \times 750 \text{ hr} = 75 \text{ kWh of energy}.$$

The same bulb, as you learned above, delivers only 2.5 W of usable light; therefore, in its lifetime it provides

$$2.50 \text{ W} \times \frac{1}{1,000} \frac{\text{kW}}{\text{W}} \times 750 \text{ hr}$$
$$= 1.88 \text{ kWh of usable light energy.}$$

To find the cost of this energy you need to find out how much your electric company charges per kilowatt hour. If you haven't already done so, find the cost of 1 kWh of electrical energy from your electric bill. Now you can determine the total cost of the energy to operate each bulb over its average lifetime. Be sure to include the original cost of the bulb. For example, suppose the 100-W bulb with an average lifetime of 750 hours cost $0.75. If electricity costs $0.10 per kilowatt hour (kWh), then the total cost of operating this bulb over its average lifetime is

$$0.100 \text{ kW} \times 750 \text{ h} \times \frac{\$0.10}{\text{kWh}} + \$0.75 = \$8.25.$$

The answer to our original question—How much light energy does the bulb provide per dollar?—can be found by dividing the total usable light energy by its cost. In our example, the bulb provides 0.228 kWh of usable light energy for a dollar because

$$\frac{1.88 \text{ kWh}}{\$8.25} = 0.228 \text{ kWh/\$.}$$

- Find the amount of usable light energy delivered per dollar by each of the bulbs in your data table. Which bulb is the best buy?
- Might two bulbs or three bulbs of lower wattage be a better buy than one higher-wattage bulb?

The best buy bulb provides the most usable light energy per dollar, but it may or may not be the most environmentally sound bulb to buy. We saw, in the calculations, that a 100-W bulb delivers only 2.50 W of usable energy. Since efficiency is the ratio of the useful energy output to the total energy input, this bulb is not very efficient. In fact, its efficiency is only

$$\frac{2.50W}{100W} \times 100 = 2.5\%.$$

- Which bulb in your data table is the most efficient?
- Compare the efficiency of a 100-W incandescent bulb with that of a 100-W fluorescent bulb.
- Which 100-W bulb is the better buy, the incandescent or the fluorescent?

ARE COMPACT FLUORESCENT BULBS A BETTER BUY?

If possible, examine some compact fluorescent bulbs. These bulbs, which can be used in place of incandescent bulbs in many light fixtures, are low-wattage bulbs that have relatively large lumens per watt ratios. For example, a Philips SL 18 bulb is an 18-W compact fluorescent bulb that provides 1,100 lumens—a ratio of 61 lumens per watt. A 75-W incandescent bulb might provide 1180 lumens, which is a ratio of only 16 lumens per watt. Furthermore, fluorescent bulbs have a lifetime of 10,000 hours or more.

It's obvious from the previous data that these bulbs are much more efficient than incandescent bulbs. But before you conclude they are a better buy than incandescent bulbs that produce comparable amounts of light, you should know that they may cost as much as $20 per bulb.

Examine some compact fluorescent bulbs and the packages they come in. After you have collected the necessary information, determine whether or not one of these bulbs, despite its price, is the best buy light bulb.

ELECTRICITY AND OHM'S LAW

Materials needed: • 10-ohm and 15-ohm resistors • small cups, such as medicine cups • water • wires with alligator clips • four (4) D-cells • cardboard tube • metal tabs • large, wide rubber band • ammeter, 0–1 ampere (A) • voltmeter, 0–10 or 0–15 volts (V)

Early in the nineteenth century, Georg Ohm, a German physicist, investigated the relationship between the voltage across a length of wire and the current (rate of charge flow) through the wire. You can do an experiment similar to the one carried out by Ohm.

To begin your experiment, place a 10-ohm resistor in a small cup of water as shown in Figure 16. (A resistor consists of a piece of thin wire, often coiled, that is enclosed in insulating material.) The water will keep the resistor at a temperature that is reasonably constant. Using insulated wires with alligator clips, connect the resistor to a battery made from four D-cells (flashlight batteries) as shown in Figure 16. The battery has a metal tab between successive cells arranged in series so that you can tap one, two, three, or all four D-cells.

One side of the battery is connected to the resistor through a 0–1 Amp DC-ammeter, which is used to measure the electric current, in units called amperes. (An ampere [A] of current is equal to a charge flow of 1 coulomb, or 6.25×10^{18} electrons, every second.) The voltage is measured with a 0–10 or 0–15 Volt DC-voltmeter. The terminals of the voltmeter are connected to the ends of the resistor as shown. Be sure that the wires to the meters are connected properly. The negative ($-$) terminal of the ammeter should be connected to the negative end of the battery. The positive terminal of the voltmeter should be connected to the end of the resistor that leads to the positive terminal of the battery.

Begin by connecting the circuit (resistor and meters) to one D-Cell in order to establish a voltage of about 1.5

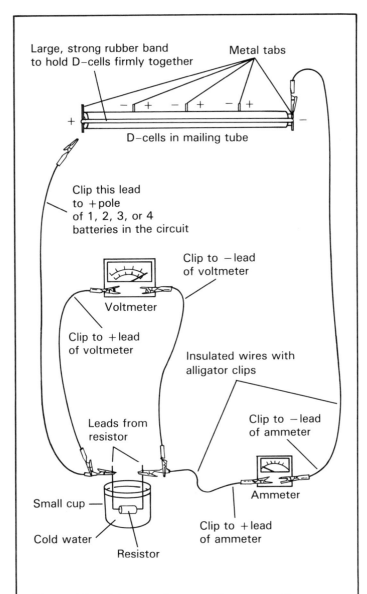

Large, strong rubber band to hold D-cells firmly together

Metal tabs

D-cells in mailing tube

Clip this lead to +pole of 1, 2, 3, or 4 batteries in the circuit

Clip to −lead of voltmeter

Voltmeter

Clip to +lead of voltmeter

Insulated wires with alligator clips

Leads from resistor

Clip to −lead of ammeter

Ammeter

Clip to +lead of ammeter

Small cup

Cold water

Resistor

Figure 16. This experiment will measure the voltage across and the current through a resistor at the same time.

V across the resistor. (You can read the voltage on the voltmeter.) Read the meters and record the current, in amperes (A), and the voltage, in volts (V).

Increase the voltage by connecting the circuit to two, three, and finally four D-cells. Each time you increase the number of cells connected to the resistor, read the meters and record the current and voltage for each trial. Once you have collected the data, disconnect the circuit.

Plot a graph of the voltage, in volts (V), along the horizontal axis and the corresponding current, in amperes (A), along the vertical axis.

- Why is the voltage plotted on the horizontal axis?
- What can you conclude about the relationship between voltage and current for this 10-ohm resistor at a reasonably constant temperature?
- Write an equation that summarizes the graph you have made.
- Repeat the experiment using a 15-ohm resistor. Are the results similar?

Ohm investigated a great variety of materials. He found that for all metallic materials the mathematical relationship between voltage and current was the same as the relationship you found for 10- and 15-ohm resistors. His discovery was summarized in a form known today as Ohm's law.

- How would you express Ohm's law?

ELECTRICAL RESISTANCE, LENGTH, AREA, AND TEMPERATURE

As you've seen, Ohm discovered that the current flowing through a metallic wire at a *constant* temperature is proportional to the voltage across the wire. This relationship, known as Ohm's law, is often expressed as

$$V = IR \ (\text{or} \ R = \frac{V}{I})$$

where V is the voltage, in volts (V), and I is the current, in amperes (A). R is defined as the *resistance* of the wire to the flow of charge. The units of resistance are ohms (Ω), where $1 \ \Omega = 1$ V/A.

Using the equipment in the previous investigation and several 10-ohm resistors, design and conduct an experiment to find out how the resistance of a wire is related to its length. (Remember, a 10-ohm resistor contains a fixed length of wire.)

- How is the resistance of the wire related to its length?

You might reason that the resistance of a wire is related to its thickness or cross-sectional area as well as its length since they both affect how easily current will pass through it. You can investigate this effect by connecting two resistors side by side (in parallel) as shown in Figure 17. (Be sure each resistor is in water.)

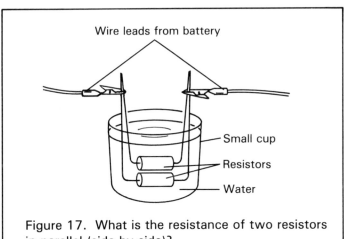

Figure 17. What is the resistance of two resistors in parallel (side by side)?

- What happens to the total cross-sectional area of the resistor wires when two of them are connected in parallel?
- How is the resistance of a wire related to its cross-sectional area?

You could probably design an experiment to test the effect of temperature on the resistance of a wire, but it might be rather tedious to carry out. Such experiments have been done, and the results for one kind of wire are given in Table 19.

Plot a graph of the resistance of the wire as a function of temperature.

Table 19: The Effect of Temperature on the Resistance of Gauge 14 Copper Wire

Temperature (°C)	Resistance (Ω/100 m)
0	0.763
20	0.828
50	0.926
75	1.007
100	1.088

- Over this small temperature range, is the relationship between resistance and temperature linear or nonlinear?
- Extrapolate (extend) your graph. What would you expect the resistance of the wire to be at 120°C? At − 20°C?
- Write the equation for the graph you have drawn. According to your equation, what is the resistance of the wire at 120°C? At − 20°C?

ELECTRICAL RESISTIVITY

Ohm discovered, as you probably have, that at a given temperature the resistance of a wire is proportional to its length and inversely proportional to its area of cross section. This is true of any metallic wire, but the actual resistance depends on the kind of wire. A Nichrome wire, for example, has a greater resistance than a copper wire of the same length and diameter. Suppose, at room temperature, you measured the resistance of copper and Nichrome wires of the same length and diameter, say a length of 1.0 m and a diameter of 0.36 mm. You would find that the resistance of the copper wire is 0.17 ohm, while the resistance of the Nichrome wire is 10 ohms—nearly 60 times the copper wire's resistance.

Knowing the resistance of a metal wire, R, and the fact that any wire's resistance is proportional to its length, L, and inversely proportional to its area of cross section, A, you may write

$$R = k\frac{L}{A}.$$

The proportionality constant, k, is defined as the resistivity of that particular metal. As you can see, the resistivity of a metal wire is proportional to its resistance. Because resistivity depends only on the material of the wire, it allows us to compare the resistance of different materials to the flow of electric charge without having to consider their particular sizes or shapes.

Table 20 gives the electrical resistivities of a number of different materials—conductors, semiconductors, and insulators.

- Which substance listed in Table 20 offers the greatest resistance to the flow of electric charge?
- Which substance in Table 20 is the best conductor of electric charge?
- On the basis of all the data in Table 20, how might you distinguish among conductors, semiconductors, and insulators?
- Suppose you have spools of gold and silver wires of

the same diameter. How should the lengths of these gold and silver wires compare if they are to have the same resistance?

• Why do you think copper wire is more commonly the wire of choice in electric circuits even though silver is a better conductor?

Table 20: The Electrical Resistivities of a Number of Metallic Conductors, Semiconductors, and Insulators

Substance	Resistivity (Ω-m at 20°C)
Conductors	
Aluminum	2.6×10^{-8}
Copper	1.7×10^{-8}
Gold	2.4×10^{-8}
Iron	9.7×10^{-8}
Lead	22×10^{-8}
Mercury	94×10^{-8}
Nichrome	100×10^{-8}
Silver	1.6×10^{-8}
Steel	20×10^{-8}
Tin	11×10^{-8}
Semiconductors	
Carbon	3.5×10^{-5}
Germanium	0.60
Silicon	$2,300$
Insulators	
Amber	5×10^{14}
Glass	$10^{10} - 10^{14}$
Lucite	$> 10^{13}$
Sulfur	2×10^{15}
Wood	$10^8 - 10^{11}$

ELECTRICAL RESISTIVITY AND THERMAL CONDUCTIVITY

The electrical resistivity of a material is an indication of how much it resists the flow of electric charge. As you

Table 21: Thermal Conductivity of a Number of Metals

Metal	Thermal Conductivity (W/m/°C)
Aluminum	237
Copper	401
Gold	318
Iron	80
Lead	35
Mercury	8
Silver	429
Tin	67

can see from Table 20, aluminum and gold wires of the same diameter and length offer very nearly the same resistance to the flow of charge. Lead, on the other hand, offers nearly ten times as much resistance to charge flow as gold and aluminum. The electrical conductivity of a material, which is a measure of how well it conducts electric charge, is simply the inverse of its resistivity.

The rate at which heat flows along a material is given by its thermal conductivity, which depends only on the nature of the material through which the heat flows. The units of thermal conductivity are energy flow per second (watts), per unit length (m) of wire, per degree of temperature change along the wire (°C), or

$$\frac{W/m}{°C}, \text{ which is the same as } \frac{W}{m-°C}$$

Table 21 lists the thermal conductivities for a number of metals. The electrical resistivities of these metals can be found in Table 20. Plot a graph of thermal conductivity versus electrical resistivity for these metals.

- What functional relationship between electrical resistivity and thermal conductivity is suggested by the graph? Draw another graph to confirm the relationship that you think may exist between these two variables.

- Did the graph confirm the relationship you predicted?
- What can you conclude about the thermal and electrical conductivities of metals?
- A prediction: Use the data in Table 21 to list the metals in that table in order of increasing electrical resistivity. Then compare your list with the metals in Table 20. How well did you do?

HEAT AND SPECIFIC HEAT

Materials needed: • string • metal washers (about 50 g) • balance • cooking pan • water • safety goggles • stove • insulated cup, 6- or 7-oz • thermometer, −10 to 110°C or −20 to 50°C (0°–120°F)

A calorie (cal) is defined as the amount of heat needed to change the temperature of 1.0 g of water by 1°C. If the temperature of 100 g of water changes by 10°C, we say that 1,000 cal of heat has been added to, or lost by, the water.

The specific heat of a substance is defined as the amount of heat needed to raise or lower the temperature of 1.0 g of the substance by 1°C. The specific heat of water, therefore, is 1.0 cal/g/°C. The specific heats of substances other than water have been determined experimentally. One way to do this is to add a known mass of the material in question, at a known temperature, to a mass of water at a different temperature.

To see how this works, tie a string around a stack of metal washers that have a mass of about 50 g. Place the washers in a cooking pan and add enough water to cover the washers. *Put on safety goggles* before you place the pan on a stove burner. Be sure the string extends over the edge of the pan, but *keep it away from the burner* where it might catch on fire.

While the water is heating, pour about 50 ml of cold tap water into a 6- or 7-ounce insulated cup. When the water in the pan starts to boil, you can check its temperature with a lab thermometer *only if* the thermometer has a range of − 10 to 110°C. If the upper range of your thermometer is only 50°C (120° F), you may assume the temperature of the boiling water to be 100°C.

Use the thermometer to find the temperature of the cold water. Record this temperature. Then use the string to pull the washers from the boiling water and quickly transfer them to the cold water. Stir the cold water as it is warmed by the washers and record the final temperature.

- What was the temperature change of the cold water? How many calories of heat did the washers transfer to the water?

You can now calculate the specific heat of the washers. Suppose, for example, that the water temperature was initially 20°C and that it rose to 30°C after the washers were added. The washers must have transferred 500 cal of heat to the water (50 g × 10°C × 1.0 cal/g/°C). In so doing, the temperature of the washers changed by 70°C (100°C − 30°C). Since the specific heat of the washers is the amount of heat needed to change 1.0 g of washers by 1.0°C, their specific heat, s, is

$$500 \text{ cal/50 g/70°C} = 0.14 \text{ cal/g/°C}.$$

- According to your data, what is the specific heat of the washers you used?

EXPANSION

Materials needed: • strip of clear plastic tape • aluminum foil • scissors • forceps • candle and candle holder • matches

As you probably know, most substances expand when heated. That is why there are gaps in railroad tracks and bridges. If not for the gaps, the long metal rails would buckle or bend on hot summer days. As you can see from Table 22, not all substances expand by the same amount per degree of temperature change. In the table, the coefficient of linear expansion is the change in length per unit length of material per degree. The coefficient of volume expansion is the change in volume per unit volume of the material per degree. For example, if a metal rod 1.0 m long expands by 1.0 mm (0.001 m) when it is heated through 100°C, its linear coefficient of expansion, α, is

$$\alpha = \frac{1.0 \times 10^{-3} \text{ m}/1.0 \text{ m}}{100°C}$$
$$= 1.0 \times 10^{-5}/°C \text{ or } 10 \times 10^{-6}/°C.$$

Because metals expand as the temperature rises, there must be gaps between the rails in railroad tracks. If not for gaps on either end, the long metal rails would buckle or bend on hot summer days.

Table 22: Coefficients of Expansion for Various Materials at 20°C

Material	Linear Coefficient ($\times 10^{-6}/°C$)	Volume Coefficient ($\times 10^{-6}/°C$)
Metallic solids		
Aluminum	24	72
Copper	17	51
Iron	12	36
Lead	29	87
Magnesium	26	78
Nickel	13	39
Zinc	25	75
Other solids		
Glass (ordinary)	9	27
Pyrex glass	3	9
Quartz	0.4	1.2
Concrete	12	36
Liquids		
Ethanol		750
Gasoline		960
Glycerine		490
Mercury		180
Gases (at constant pressure)		
Air		3,670
Argon		3,660
Carbon dioxide		3,740
Helium		3,665
Hydrogen		3,660

One thing you can do to illustrate the differences in expansion due to heating is to use scissors to cut strips of identical size (about 1.3 cm × 8 cm) from aluminum foil and clear plastic tape. Fasten the clear tape to the dull side of the aluminum foil. Then, *under adult supervision,* use forceps to hold one end of the two-layered strip well above a candle flame so that its temperature will increase without burning the tape.

- What happens as the temperature of the strip increases?
- Does it matter which side is closer to the flame?
- How can you tell that the plastic tape expands more than the aluminum when heated through the same temperature change?
- Why are linear coefficients for liquids and gases not listed in the table?
- Roughly, how do the expansions of solids, liquids, and gases compare?
- How do the volume coefficients of expansion compare with the linear coefficients? Can you explain this ratio? If not, consider a hypothetical rod 100 units long that expands by 1 unit when the temperature rises 1 degree. Its linear coefficient of expansion is 0.01. Now imagine the same material as a cube 100 units on a side. What will be its volume coefficient of expansion? How does this compare with its linear coefficient? The ratio can be proved algebraically by considering the length to be L and the increase in length per degree to be ΔL. What are the steps in your proof?
- Mercury freezes at $-39°C$. If mercury were frozen in the shape of long rods, what do you predict its linear coefficient of expansion would be? What assumptions have you made?
- What do you notice about the coefficients of expansion for gases?
- Can you explain why the volume coefficients for various liquids and solids differ while those for all gases are very nearly equal?
- Give one reason why iron (or steel) rods are used in reinforced concrete.

CHEMISTRY AND MATHEMATICS

For many years after Thomas Dalton proposed the theory that matter was made up of atoms and that all the atoms of an element were identical with each other but different from the atoms of any other element, chemists could find only the *relative* masses of these atoms. They knew that oxygen atoms were 16 times as massive as hydrogen atoms and half as massive as sulfur atoms, but they did not know the actual mass of any atom. Techniques that enabled them to determine the actual masses of atoms were developed about the turn of the twentieth century. Since that time much has been learned about atoms and how they behave.

In this chapter, you'll examine information about the atomic masses of elements and their specific heats to see whether you can arrive at the same mathematical generalization that Dulong and Petit did more than 150 years ago. Then, you'll examine some constants pertaining to the first 20 elements in the periodic table to see whether you can discover any patterns. You will explore the properties of substances known as the saturated hydrocarbons, and you'll see how their similarities enable you to predict the properties of other saturated hydrocarbons. Then you'll carry out your own investigation to find out whether the relationship between the index of refraction and the density of hydrocarbons holds for other substances.

THE DISCOVERY OF DULONG AND PETIT

Early in the nineteenth century, two French scientists, Pierre Louis Dulong and Alexis Petit, discovered an interesting relationship between the specific heat of a substance and its atomic mass. At that time, only the relative masses of atoms had been determined. It was known that oxygen atoms were 16 times as massive as hydrogen atoms, but the true masses of the atoms were unknown. This is not surprising since the actual mass of a hydrogen atom is only 1.66×10^{-24} g.

Table 23 lists a number of elements together with their specific heats and relative atomic masses.

- From the data in the table, what happens to the specific heat of elements as their atomic mass increases?

One way to see whether a relationship exists is to plot the inverse of the specific heat for each element listed as a function of the atomic mass. Another approach, which seems to have been the one used by Dulong and Petit, is to compare the product of specific heat and atomic (or molecular) mass for each of the elements. Place a piece of paper beside Table 23 and prepare a new column on the paper in which you record the product (atomic mass × specific heat) for each element listed. After you have done this, find the average value of this product and then state the law of Dulong and Petit in your own words.

Before Dulong and Petit made their discovery, people wondered why specific heat varied so much from one

Table 23: The Relative Atomic Masses and Specific Heats of a Number of Elements

Element	Relative Atomic or Molecular Mass	Specific Heat (cal/g/°C)
Aluminum (Al)	27	0.22
Argon (Ar)	40	0.12
Arsenic (As)	75	0.079
Copper (Cu)	64	0.092
Hydrogen (H_2)	2	3.4
Iron (Fe)	56	0.11
Lead (Pb)	207	0.031
Magnesium (Mg)	24	0.25
Mercury (Hg)	201	0.033
Nickel (Ni)	59	0.11
Nitrogen (N_2)	28	0.25
Oxygen (O_2)	32	0.22
Phosphorus (P)	31	0.19
Silver (Ag)	108	0.056
Sodium (Na)	23	0.29
Sulfur (S)	32	0.17
Zinc (Zn)	65	0.094

Note: Elements such as hydrogen whose molecules normally consist of two atoms are written with a subscript 2, as in H_2. The atomic masses of such elements are half their molecular mass.

substance to another. Because specific heat is a measure of the heat needed to raise the temperature of 1 g of material 1° C, it is not a comparison of equal numbers of atoms or molecules. A gram of aluminum and a gram of zinc, or a gram of any other element, do not contain the same number of atoms. Zinc atoms are heavier than aluminum atoms (65 versus 27), so there are fewer atoms in a gram of zinc than in a gram of aluminum. To obtain samples of different elements with equal numbers of atoms (or molecules), we can weigh out masses that have the same ratio as the relative atomic (or molecular) masses of the elements—65 g of zinc and 27 g of aluminum, for example.

- Why would this ratio assure us of equal numbers of atoms of zinc and aluminum?

    A sample of an element (or compound) that has a mass in grams equal to its atomic (or molecular) mass is defined as 1 *mole* of the substance. All such samples contain the same number of atoms or molecules—6.02×10^{23}. In other words, 65 g of zinc, 27 g of aluminum, 108 g of silver, and so on, all contain 6.02×10^{23} atoms.

- What additional information had to be known before it could be determined that a mole of any substance contains 6.02×10^{23} atoms?

- You learned earlier that the mass of a hydrogen atom is 1.66×10^{-24} g and that its relative atomic mass is 1. Use this information to show that a mole of hydrogen (1.00 g) contains 6.02×10^{23} atoms.

Heat capacity is defined as the amount of heat required to change the temperature of a sample of matter by 1° C. Thus, the heat capacity of 100 g of water is 100 cal/°C. The molar heat capacity is the amount of heat required to change the temperature of 1 mole of a substance 1°C. For example, a mole of aluminum contains 27 g. Since 0.22 cal is required to raise the temperature of 1.0 g of aluminum 1.0°C, the molar heat capacity of aluminum is given by

$$(0.22 \text{ cal/g/°C}) (27 \text{ g/mole}) = 5.9 \text{ cal/mole/°C.}$$

- Why are the numbers in the new column that you calculated before equal to the molar heat capacities of the elements listed in Table 23? What do these numbers indicate about the heat required to raise *equal* numbers of atoms (or molecules) of *different* elements through the same temperature change?

- What could you do to find out whether the law of Dulong and Petit applies to compounds as well as elements?

ATOMIC CONSTANTS

Table 24 lists a number of atomic constants for the first 20 elements in the periodic table. The atomic number (the order in which the elements are listed) is the number of protons in the element's nucleus. The molar volume is the volume that a mole (6.02×10^{23} atoms) of the element occupies in the solid or liquid state. The atomic radius is an estimate based on a number of factors, and

Table 24: Some Constants for the First 20 Elements of the Periodic Table

Element	Atomic number	Molar volume (cm^3)	Atomic radius $\times 10^{-12}m$	First ionization energy (eV)
Hydrogen	1	13.26	37	13.6
Helium	2	32.07	50	24.5
Lithium	3	13.00	152	5.4
Beryllium	4	4.88	111	9.3
Boron	5	4.62	88	8.3
Carbon	6	3.42	77	11.3
Nitrogen	7	13.65	70	14.5
Oxygen	8	8.00	66	13.6
Fluorine	9	18.05	64	17.3
Neon	10	13.97	70	21.5
Sodium	11	23.68	186	5.1
Magnesium	12	13.98	160	7.6
Aluminum	13	10.00	143	6.0
Silicon	14	12.06	117	8.1
Phosphorus	15	17.02	110	10.9
Sulfur	16	15.49	104	10.3
Chlorine	17	17.46	99	13.0
Argon	18	24.12	94	15.7
Potassium	19	45.36	231	4.3
Calcium	20	25.86	197	6.1

the first ionization energy is the energy required to remove the first electron from a neutral atom in the gaseous state. The energy is given in electron volts (eV). An electron volt is 1.6×10^{-19} joules (J).

Use the data in Table 24 to make a graph of the first ionization energies as a function of the atomic number for the first 20 elements. Connect the points with straight lines.

Next, make a graph of the atomic radii as a function of the atomic number. Keep the same spacing for atomic numbers on both graphs.

- Compare the two graphs. How are they related? How might you explain this relationship?

  The elements lithium, sodium and potassium are the first three members of a family of elements known as the *alkali metals*.
- How do the atomic radii of these elements compare with the atomic radii of elements that precede and follow each of them in atomic number? (For example, in the case of sodium, compare its atomic radius with those of neon and magnesium.)
- How do their first ionization energies compare with those of their neighbors? Their molar volumes? Do their molar volumes seem to reflect their atomic radii?
- What do you notice about the differences between the atomic numbers of these three alkali metals?

  The next two elements in the alkali metal family are rubidium and cesium. Rubidium has an atomic number of 37, a molar volume of 55.79 cm³, an atomic radius of 244×10^{-12} m, and a first ionization energy of 4.2 eV. Cesium has an atomic number of 55, a molar volume of 70.96 cm³, an atomic radius of 262×10^{-12} m, and a first ionization energy of 3.9 eV.

- Do the trends in atomic size, volume, and first ionization energy continue with these next two members of the alkali metal family? How about the differences in atomic number?
- The density of lithium is 0.534 g/cm^3. Calculate the mass of a lithium atom in grams.
- In Table 23 you saw that the atomic mass of aluminum is 27; that means a mole of aluminum has a mass of 27 g. Using that information and the molar volume of aluminum in Table 24, what is the density of aluminum? What is the mass of one atom of aluminum?

SOME PROPERTIES OF HYDROCARBONS

Carbon and hydrogen combine to form a great many compounds. One of the simplest of these compounds is methane—the principal constituent of natural gas—which is used as a fuel throughout the world. Its chemical formula is CH_4.

Adding an additional carbon and two hydrogen atoms to the methane molecule gives us ethane, C_2H_6. Adding yet another CH_2 group to ethane forms propane, C_3H_8. This procedure of adding CH_2 groups can be continued to form compounds with four, five, six, and so on, carbon atoms, as shown in Table 25. All of these substances, which are called the saturated hydrocarbons, are found in petroleum. The compounds are separated from each other by distillation in huge oil refineries built by petroleum companies. Saturated hydrocarbons are the basic ingredient for many chemical industries.

- From the data in Table 25, draw a graph of density as a function of the number of carbon atoms in each hydrocarbon. Use the graph to estimate the density of nonane, C_9H_{20}. If your library has a copy of *The Handbook of Chemistry and Physics*, you can check your estimate.

*Hydrocarbons come from crude oil,
which is pumped from the earth by oil wells
like this one near Osage, Wyoming.*

- Use the same graph to estimate the density of penta-decane, $C_{15}H_{32}$. Check this estimate against the handbook value. How close was your estimate?
- Use the same graphical methods of interpolation and extrapolation to estimate the melting and boiling points of nonane and pentadecane. Then check your estimates against the handbook values. How close were your estimates?
- A substance is chemically analyzed and found to contain only the elements carbon and hydrogen. Experiments indicate that its boiling point is $-0.5°C$ and its melting point is $-138°C$. What do you think the substance is? What would you do to confirm its identity?
- Which of the saturated hydrocarbons in Table 25 are liquids at room temperature? Which are gases? Are any of them solids at room temperature?

Table 25: Some Properties of the First Ten Saturated Hydrocarbons

Chemical Formula	Name of Chemical	Mass per Mole (g/mole)	Density (g/cm³)	Melting Point (°C)	Boiling Point (°C)	Index of Refraction (n)	Heat of Combustion (J/mole × 10⁶)
CH_4	methane	16	0.466	−182.6	−164.0	—	0.891
C_2H_6	ethane	30	0.572	−183.3	−88.6	1.0377	1.56
C_3H_8	propane	44	0.585	−189.7	−42.1	1.2898	2.22
C_4H_{10}	butane	58	0.601	−138.4	−0.5	1.3543	2.86
C_5H_{12}	pentane	72	0.620	−130.0	36.1	1.3575	3.54
C_6H_{14}	hexane	86	0.660	−95.0	69.0	1.3751	4.16
C_7H_{16}	heptane	100	0.684	−90.6	98.4	1.3878	4.81
C_8H_{18}	octane	114	0.702	−56.8	125.7	1.3974	5.45
$C_{10}H_{22}$	decane	142	0.730	−29.7	174.1	1.4102	6.74

Note: The densities are for the liquid state at 20°C or, for those substances that are gases at 20°C, at temperatures close to the boiling point.

HYDROCARBONS AND HEATS OF COMBUSTION

The molar heat of combustion of a substance, ΔH_c, is the energy released when 1 mole of the compound burns completely. The chemical equation for the complete combustion of methane is

$$CH_4 + 2O_2 \rightarrow CO_2 + 2H_2O + 891{,}000 \text{ J.}$$

In Table 25, the heats of combustion of the hydrocarbons are given in millions of joules per mole. As you can see from the table, the heats of combustion increase with the size of the hydrocarbon molecules. Is there a simple mathematical relationship between the heats of combustion and the number of carbon atoms in the molecules?

To find out, make a graph of the heat of combustion as a function of the number of carbon atoms for each of the hydrocarbons listed in Table 25.

• Is there a relationship between the heat of combustion and the number of carbon atoms in the saturated hydrocarbon? If there is, what equation best describes it?

Methane and propane are two hydrocarbons that are used as fuels.
- From the third column in Table 25, you can find the molar masses of methane and propane. Calculate the heats of combustion for these two gases in joules per gram (J/g) rather than joules per mole (J/mole). How do they compare?

In transporting fuels, volume is generally a more important factor than mass. Consequently, in deciding whether to ship methane or propane over large distances it would be useful to know the energy that can be obtained per unit volume of these two gases.
- Using the densities given in column four of Table 25, how can you find the volume of 1 gram of methane? Of 1 gram of propane? What are these volumes?
- What is the heat of combustion of methane in joules per cubic centimeter (J/cm^3)? Of propane? Which gas is more economical to ship in terms of the energy it provides per volume?

The absolute or Kelvin temperature scale is often used in science because it has no negative values. Its zero point, which is at $-273°C$, is the lowest temperature possible. Since the size of a degree on the Kelvin scale, $T(K)$, is the same as a degree on the Celsius scale, $T(°C)$, it's easy to convert from the Celsius to the Kelvin scale:

$$T(K) = T(°C) + 273.$$

Notice that the Kelvin scale does not express temperature in degrees. Thus, $0°C = 273K$, $100°C = 373K$, $273°C = 546K$, and $-273°C = 0K$.

- The molar volume of a substance is the volume occupied by 1 mole of the substance. What is the molar volume of each of the substances listed in Table 25?
- Are the molar volumes of the saturated hydrocarbons proportional to their boiling temperatures? How can you avoid using negative temperatures to find the answer to this question?

INDEX OF REFRACTION AND DENSITY

In Chapter 2, you found that the index of refraction, n, for a transparent substance is given by

$$n = \frac{\sin i}{\sin r}$$

where i is the angle of incidence, which is usually measured in air or a vacuum, and r is the angle of refraction, which is measured in the transparent medium.

- Using the data in Table 25, plot a graph of index of refraction versus density for those hydrocarbons that are liquids at room temperature.
- On the basis of the graph you have drawn, does there seem to be a linear relationship between index of refraction and density for the saturated hydrocarbons that are liquids at room temperature?
- On the basis of your earlier estimate of the density of nonane, C_9H_{20}, what would you predict is the index of refraction of nonane?
- Why do you think no index is given for methane?

INDEX OF REFRACTION AND DENSITY
FOR OTHER SUBSTANCES

Materials needed: • black construction paper "ray maker" • clear, rectangular, plastic box • water • dark room • lamp • small protractor • white paper • ruler • sheet of cardboard • graduated cylinder • balance

Does the linear relationship between density and index of refraction that you found for the liquid hydrocarbons extend to all liquid substances? You can find out by using the same materials you used to investigate refraction in Chapter 2. Carry out experiments to see whether there is a linear relationship between index of refraction and density for a number of common liquids. To find the index of refraction, you can simply measure the angles of incidence and refraction for a reasonably large angle, say 30 degrees, and then calculate the index from the ratio of the sines of the angles.

- Why should you choose a reasonably large angle to measure?

    You can find the density of the liquids by calculating the mass to volume ratio for each of them. Masses can be found by using a balance. The volumes can be measured with a graduated cylinder.

- Determine the index of refraction and density for several common liquids. You might investigate water, rubbing alcohol, glycol (antifreeze), and a concentrated salt solution. *Alcohol is flammable. Keep it away from flames. Both alcohol and glycol are poisonous. Keep them away from your mouth.*

Once you've collected the data, you can plot the indices of refraction as a function of the corresponding densities to see whether there is a linear relationship between them. You might also like to add the materials listed in Table 26 to your graph. The indices and densities of these materials, which are more difficult to obtain or are toxic, were, like yours, determined at room temperature.

- For the materials in Table 26 and the common ones that you investigated, does there seem to be a mathematical relationship between density and index of refraction?

Table 26: The Refractive Indices and Densities of a Number of Liquids and Solids

Substance	Index of Refraction	Density (g/cm^3)
Ethyl alcohol	1.36	0.79
Carbon disulfide	1.63	1.26
Glycerine	1.47	1.26
Oleic acid	1.46	0.60

7

ASTRONOMY AND MATHEMATICS

As you have seen, the mathematics needed to describe atomic sizes involves numbers that are very small. Astronomers, on the other hand, require numbers that are very large as they investigate the distances to planets within the solar system or to galaxies that are light-years away.

In this chapter you'll find the mathematical patterns that govern the distances between sun and planets, as well as those found in the paths of moons around planets and planets around the sun. You will learn, too, of the particles (asteroids) that may be the remains of a missing planet, particles that cross earth's orbit. You'll try to predict the probability of one of the larger asteroids colliding with the earth.

DISTANCES TO THE PLANETS

The Bode-Titius law or rule was designed by Johann Bode in the eighteenth century to help people remember the distances of the planets from the sun. The distances are given in astronomical units (AU); 1 AU is the distance

The distances between earth, moon, and sun are such that when the moon passes between the earth and the sun, the tip of the moon's dark shadow just barely reaches the earth's surface. The result is a solar eclipse, such as the one shown here.

from the earth to the sun. The rule produces a progression of distances through the following three steps:

1. Write down the following sequence of numbers: 0, 3, 6, 12, 24, 48, 96, 192, 384, 768. (Notice that each number after 3 is simply twice the preceding number.)
2. Add 4 to each number in the sequence.
3. Divide each sum by 10.

- How do the values for the planetary distances obtained from the Bode-Titius progression compare with the measured values given in Table 27?

Table 27: The Distances from the Sun to the Planets Discovered Before 1781

Planet	Distance to Planet from Sun (AU)
Mercury	0.39
Venus	0.72
Earth	1.0ᶜ
Mars	1.52
Jupiter	5.20
Saturn	9.54

- Some astronomers believed that Bode's rule was simply a mnemonic device for remembering the distances to the planets. Others felt it was a scientific law that could be used to predict the distances to undiscovered planets. Why did the latter group of astronomers search for a planet between Mars and Jupiter? Where did they expect to find it?

The planet Uranus, at a distance of 19.18 AU from the sun, was discovered by William Herschel in 1781. In 1846, Johann Galle turned his telescope to a position predicted by John C. Adams and Urbain Leverrier and saw the planet Neptune. It was 30.06 AU from the sun. The last planet to be discovered was Pluto, which was first seen by Clyde Tombaugh in 1930. Pluto was 39.44 AU from the sun.

- Would Bode's law have helped astronomers to locate Uranus? Neptune? Pluto?

ASTEROIDS

As early as 1772, Bode suggested that there must be a planet between the orbits of Mars and Jupiter. He did this by using his numerical "law" that predicted the radii of the planetary orbits. You saw the predictions of Bode's

The Barringer Crater, located near Winslow, Arizona, has a diameter of 1.2 km. It is believed to have been made by an asteroid about 35 m in diameter that struck the earth about 25,000 years ago.

law in the previous section. Although Bode predicted a planet at 2.8 AU from the sun, no such planet had been found. Later, a magnificent band of planetary fragments, called asteroids, was found in this region. Continued study over the years has revealed that a very large number of asteroids are found throughout the solar system, although most of these planetesimals are indeed found between the orbits of Mars and Jupiter. This asteroid belt consists of some million objects that are at least 1 kilometer (km) in diameter.

Table 28 shows the distribution of approximately 2,300 catalogued asteroids that are found between the orbits of Mars, at 1.5 AU, and Jupiter, at 5.2 AU.

Table 28: Asteroids in Orbit Between Mars and Jupiter

Distance (AU)	Number of Asteroids	Distance (AU)	Number of Asteroids
1.70–1.80	3	3.20–3.30	73
1.80–1.90	15	3.30–3.40	21
1.90–2.00	15	3.40–3.50	21
2.00–2.10	0	3.50–3.60	3
2.10–2.20	74	3.60–3.70	2
2.20–2.30	260	3.70–3.80	1
2.30–2.40	100	3.80–3.90	1
2.40–2.50	153	3.90–4.00	26
2.50–2.60	168	4.00–4.10	2
2.60–2.70	238	4.10–4.30	0
2.70–2.80	244	4.30–4.40	2
2.80–2.90	143	4.40–5.00	0
2.90–3.00	102	5.00–5.10	2
3.00–3.10	240	5.10–5.20	16
3.10–3.20	379	5.20–5.30	10

- Make a histogram of the data in Table 28. What light does your histogram shed on Bode's prediction that a planet would be found at 2.8 AU?

EARTH-APPROACHING OBJECTS

There are probably a thousand asteroids on the order of a kilometer in diameter that occasionally come close to the earth in their orbits. Table 29 gives some of the statistics involved in a collision between asteroids or meteoroids and the earth.

The numbers in the table are based on many assumptions. The first assumption is that each 10-fold decrease in size is accompanied by a 100-fold increase in the number of objects. This is true in the asteroid belt, but for earth-approaching objects the scaling is uncertain. Although this number is approximate, a better determination is one of the goals of the Spacewatch Camera, a sky-searching project currently under way.

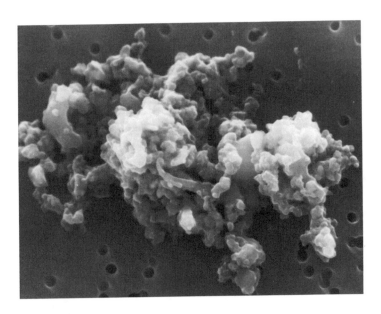

This particle, believed to be a piece of a comet, has a diameter of only 10 microns (10^{-6} m). It is one of the smaller particles that impacts with the space shuttle and the earth's atmosphere.

The impact probabilities involve astronomical estimates as well. They are derived from observations of impact cratering on the moon. The earth and the moon have certainly been subjected to the same flux, or rate of flow, of asteroidal particles through their histories. The results of the *Apollo* missions to the moon provided the evidence for the impact probabilities.

The impact energies are calculated by using the relation for kinetic energy,

$$E_k = \frac{1}{2} mv^2.$$

Here the mass, *m*, of the impacting body is found from an estimated average density of 3 g/cm³. Typical relative velocities between the earth and asteroids are 11 to 30 km/s. Knowing the mass and velocity of the asteroid enables us to use the kinetic energy equation to find the impact energy. The impact energies are expressed in terms of the amount of energy released by the Hiroshima atomic explosion in World War II. One "Hiroshima" is the equivalent of 5×10^{13} J of energy.

- Show why the impact energies decrease by factors of 1,000 as the diameters of the impactors decrease by factors of 10.
- From the column showing the frequencies of impact, find the corresponding times between impacts for asteroids of each size.

A graph of object diameters versus times between impacts will help us to understand a great deal about the history of life on earth. For example,

---

Table 29: Earth-Approaching Objects That Have Struck the Earth

Object Diameter (km)	Number of Objects in Asteroid Belt	Impact Frequency (/year)	Impact Energy (Hiroshimas)	Evidence or Example of Object
10	10	10^{-8}	10^9	Crater in Sudbury, Ontario
1	1,000	10^{-6}	10^6	—
0.1	100,000	10^{-4}	10^3	Arizona's Barringer Crater
0.001	Very large	1	10^{-3}	Meteorites
10^{-6}	Very large	10^6	–	Impactors on the surface of the space shuttle

Source: E. Shoemaker, Physics Today (July 1987): 27, and (February 1985): 3.

were the dinosaurs extinguished by a collision of an asteroid with the earth? This theory is often advanced to explain their disappearance. If such a cataclysm took place, are other such impacts likely? How often? Can we predict them, observe their beginnings, and even intercept them? First let us use some of our data to find a pattern.

- How often would you expect a 1-km space object to collide with the earth? What would be the average time between impacts for such objects?
- Make a graph of object diameters versus the time between impacts. Remember, to do this with data that cover such an enormous range, you will need to use logarithms (see chapter 2). Make each interval on both axes correspond to one power of the variable. You can label the intervals with the power of 10 that is being represented.
- The physicist Luis Alvarez proposed that approximately 65 million years ago an impactor 10 km in width struck the earth and brought an end to the age of the dinosaurs. Is such an extinction compatible with your graphic data?
- How might such a collision be prevented?

THE MOONS OF JUPITER
AND THE PLANETARY ORBITS

Galileo observed the moons of Jupiter when he first directed a 10-power telescope toward that planet in 1609. Here was the first evidence that the earth was not necessarily the center of all celestial motion.

Table 30 shows recent values for the distances of the moons of Jupiter from the planet. Notice that the distances are given in units of Jupiter radii. For example, the orbit of the Jovian moon Io is found to be about six Jupiter radii from the center of the planet. Thus, it revolves nearly five Jupiter radii above the surface of the planet.

- The orbital periods in the table refer to the time each moon takes to complete one revolution around Jupiter as measured in earth days. How do you suppose Galileo measured the orbital periods?

  Using the data in Table 30, you can discover for yourself an amazing relationship.

Table 30: The Orbital Radii and Periods of the Moons of Jupiter (Jovian Moons)

Name of Jovian Moon	Distance of Moon from Jupiter (Jupiter Radii)	Orbital Period (Days)
Almathea	2.55	0.49
Io	5.95	1.77
Europa	9.47	3.55
Ganymede	15.10	7.15
Callisto	26.60	6.70

- Find the value of the cube of the distance of Io from Jupiter. Now divide this number by the square of Io's orbital period. Follow the same procedure for each of the other moons of Jupiter. What do you find?

Does this relationship work for the moons of any planet? Table 31 gives the data for a few of the 17 or more moons of Saturn.

Table 31: The Orbital Radii and Periods of a Few of the Moons of Saturn

Name of Moon	Distance of Moon from Saturn (Saturn Radii)	Orbital Period (Days)
Janus	2.51	0.695
Calypso	4.88	1.888
Dione	6.26	2.737

- For each moon of Saturn given in Table 31, find orbital radius^3/period^2. What do you find? How is this relationship similar to what you found for the moons of Jupiter? How is it different?

Your discovery suggests applying the same analysis to the planets of the solar system, since they also revolve around a central body—the sun. Table 32 gives the orbital radii and periods for the planets. This time the radii are in astronomical units (AU), where one astronomical unit is the distance of the earth from the sun, and the periods are in years as measured on earth.

Once again, use the data in Table 32 to find the value of the following ratio for each of the planets:

$$\frac{\text{orbital radius}^3}{\text{period}^2}$$

Seven of the 17 moons of Saturn are shown here circling the planet in a montage of photographs taken by the Voyager *spacecrafts.*

Table 32: The Orbital Radii and Periods of the Planets

Name of planet	Radius of Orbit (AU)	Period (years)
Mercury	0.389	0.241
Venus	0.725	0.614
Earth	1.00	1.00
Mars	1.53	1.88
Jupiter	5.22	11.8
Saturn	9.60	29.4
Uranus	19.3	84.7
Neptune	30.2	165
Pluto	39.6	247

- What do you find? Compare your results for the planets with your results for the moons of Jupiter. What do you conclude?
- Do you think the units have any effect on the relationship, or are they merely a matter of convenience? To find out, change the periods of a few of the planets, such as earth and Mars, from years to days. Now find the ratios using these units. How do the new ratios compare with one another?

You may be interested in knowing that Sir Isaac Newton used this information in his discovery of the universal law of gravitation. Any elementary physics text will explain how he did it.

Since Galileo was able to observe the Jovian moons with a simple 10-power telescope, you should be able to do the same. If your telescope has a ruled scale on the eyepiece, you can measure the relative radii of the orbits for each of the moons. By keeping detailed data for about 6 months, you can determine the period of each of the moons and the mean radii of their orbits. Then you can use your own data to determine the value of the ratio

$$\frac{\text{orbital radius}^3}{\text{period}^2}$$

BIOLOGY, THE EARTH, AND MATHEMATICS

In this chapter you'll see a few of the ways in which mathematics is used in biology and earth science. You will learn how the basic mathematics involved in scaling can explain why small animals are not found in cold climates; how a logarithmic histogram can be used to estimate the total number of land animals; how mathematics contributes to our understanding of the greenhouse effect; and how we can estimate the number of openings in the leaves of plants.

ANIMALS AND SCALING

Materials needed: • shallow container, such as the plastic lid of a large can • regular hollow cylinder, such as a frozen juice container • freezer • ruler • stopwatch or watch or clock with second hand or second mode • bucket of water • modeling clay

In an essay entitled "On Being the Right Size," the famous biologist J. B. S. Haldane made it clear that large animals are not simply blown-up versions of smaller animals that belong to the same biological order. A rhinoceros, for example, is much heavier than a gazelle, but because the strength of bones, like the strength of ropes, depends on the area of cross section, the legs of a rhinoceros are much thicker proportionally than those of the slender-legged gazelle. He went on to say that a mouse, because it has so much surface area for its volume, "eats about one quarter its own weight of food every day, which is mainly used in keeping it warm. For the same reason small animals cannot live in cold countries."

A mouse loses (or gains) heat through its body surface. On a cold night, it does the same thing you do, it curls up into a ball to reduce the surface exposed to the cold surroundings.

To see the effect of surface area on heat flow, prepare two pieces of ice that have the same volume but different surface areas. You can do this by pouring 100 cm³ (3.5 oz) of water into a shallow container such as the plastic lid of a large container. Pour an equal volume into a regular cylinder such as a frozen juice can. Then freeze the water in both containers.

When both the ice cylinder and ice "pancake" are thoroughly frozen, remove them from the freezer. Quickly measure the diameter and height of each piece of ice. Then, as you begin recording the time, place both pieces of ice in a large bucket of water. Stir the water constantly and note the time when each piece has melted.

From your size measurements, determine the surface area and volume of each piece of ice.

- What should be the volume of each piece of ice? (Remember, water expands when it freezes to form ice, which has a density of 0.92 g/cm³.) To a reasonable degree of accuracy, do your measurements confirm this expected volume?
- What was the surface area of each piece of ice?
- How long did it take each piece to melt? How can you explain the difference in melting times?

- Would you expect the melting times to be inversely proportional to the surface areas? Why? (Remember, as the ice melts, its size decreases, and so does it surface area.)

You might think that a mouse weighing one-thousandth as much as you would require one-thousandth as much food. You would be right if the mouse also had one-thousandth as much surface area through which it loses heat—heat that has to be replaced by "burning" food. But does such a mouse have a surface area that is one-thousandth as large as yours?

This elephant obviously weighs more and has more surface area than the egret sitting on its back. But is the ratio of surface area to weight the same for each animal?

To see whether or how the ratio of surface area to volume changes with size, use some clay to make three different cubes. Make a cube that is 1 cm on a side, another that is 2 cm on a side, and a third that is 4 cm on a side.

- What are the total surface area and volume of each cube?
    Make a data table in which you record the total surface area (remember, a cube has six sides) and volume of each cube. For each cube calculate the ratio of its surface area to its volume.
- What happens to the ratio of the surface area to the volume when the length of a cube is doubled?
- What is the surface area to volume ratio of a cube 10 cm on a side? One meter on a side? What happens to the surface area to volume ratio when the length of a cube increases by a factor of 10?
- How do the results of your experiments help to explain Haldane's words "Small animals cannot live in cold countries"?

HOW MANY SPECIES INHABIT THE EARTH?

The sad truth is that no one knows. The answer is relevant to efforts to conserve biological diversity and could illuminate crucial questions about evolution and management of the environment.

This is the headline from the October 1992 lead article in *Scientific American*.

There are many reasons biologists believe it is important to find an answer to this question. On a very practical level, essentially all modern medicines have been developed from natural products. We can continue to develop new pharmaceuticals only if we continue to find out what species are available.

Every year 1 to 2 percent of the earth's tropical rain forests are being destroyed along with uncounted species that dwell there. In addition to the destruction of species in general, some biologists suspect that destruction of the rain forest has led to the release of many strains of viruses, some harmless, others potentially dangerous to humans. The destruction of any ecosystem is accompanied by a loss of species, but it also produces a population explosion among certain extremely adaptable strains of viruses—strains that can rapidly mutate. How many of these viruses are there? That depends on how many species of plants and animals there are, since all living things carry viruses.

Additionally, we want to know how biological systems work. The man-made changes in the biosphere have such a great impact on the life of this planet that we must understand how physical and biological processes are coupled. How can we learn about this coupling if we don't even know what's out there?

Finally, we explore the ecosystem for the same reason we reach out to the stars and inward to the fundamental particles of matter. The human species has an unrelenting curiosity that makes us seek to understand the universe in which we live.

There are many ways of attempting to estimate the number of species. Here is one that may or may not lead to an answer for part of the animal kingdom. Table 33 classifies land animals according to their length and number of identified species.

Make a histogram of this data by dividing the horizontal axis into equal spaces. Each space will represent a characteristic size—0.0005–0.001 m, 0.001–0.005 m, 0.005–0.01 m, and so on. The vertical axis will indicate the number of species in each size group. Because the number of species covers such a wide range, you will have to use a logarithmic scale. For each size group draw a vertical bar that represents the number of species.

Table 33: The Number of Species of Land Animals Arranged According to Size

Characteristic Size (meters)	Number of Identified Species
0.0005–0.001	26,000
0.001–0.005	420,000
0.005–0.01	740,000
0.01–0.05	150,000
0.05–0.1	10,000
0.1–0.5	7,900
0.5–1	900
1–5	360
5–10	7

Source: R.M. May, Science **241** *(1988): 1141–1149.*

• Many biologists believe that the record of catalogued species for animals of length less than about 1 centimeter (0.01 m) is far from complete. In what way does your histogram suggest that these biologists are correct?

Assuming that the biologists mentioned are correct, draw a smooth curve through the midpoints of your bar graph for sizes from 5–10 m down to 0.01–0.05 m. Then *extrapolate* the curve for sizes less than a centimeter.

• From your extrapolation, estimate the *total* number of species down to 0.0005 m in length.

Although your bar graph is for recorded species, your extrapolated graph may represent recorded *plus* unrecorded species. This is because most of the larger species are very visible and well known, and it is the larger-species portion of the graph that is used as a basis for your extrapolation. The smaller-species end of the scale marks the approximate dividing line between macroscopic and microscopic animals. So your extrapolated graph is an estimate of the total number of species of microscopic land animals based on the known number of macroscopic ones.

- Biologists refer to a rule of thumb that states that for every 10-fold reduction in length, the number of animal species increases 100 times. Does your graph verify this rule?

The system for classifying plants and animals that we use today was first proposed in 1758 by the Swedish natural scientist Carolus Linnaeus. Figure 18*a* and *b* are two graphs showing the rates of discovery for two groups of species—birds and arthropods (spiders and crustaceans, but *not* insects, which are also arthropods).

- Why do you think these two graphs are so different?

MATH AND LEAVES

Materials needed: • forceps • geranium leaf • water • eyedropper • microscope slide • cover slip • microscope • ruler, clear with dark markings • leaves from other plants

If you look closely at a leaf's "skin" you'll see tiny openings, called stomates, that allow gases to enter and leave the cells within the leaf. These openings are bordered by bean-shaped cells, appropriately called guard cells, that control the size of the openings when they swell or shrink.

To see these stomates, fold a geranium leaf and use forceps to peel away a small section of the leaf's lower epidermis. Mount the tissue in a drop of water on a microscope slide, add a glass cover slip, and examine the tissue under a microscope. Once you can identify the stomates, examine other sections of the same leaf tissue

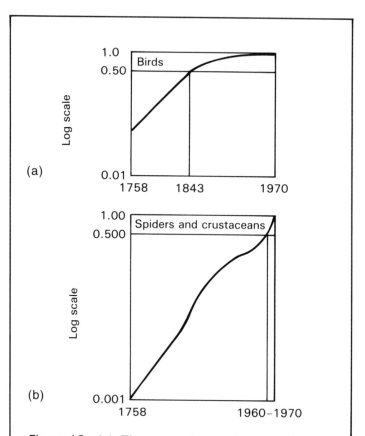

Figure 18. (a) The curve shows the rate of discovery of bird species from 1758 to 1970. The number of known species is shown as a fraction on a logarithmic scale of the total number known in 1970. The intersection of the vertical and horizontal lines shows the point when half the total number of species known in 1970 had been discovered. (b) Similarly, this graph shows the known species of spiders and crustaceans (essentially, arthropods excluding insects) from 1758 to 1970. The pattern of discovery is very different from that for bird species. Half of the total up to 1970 has been recorded since 1960.

under the microscope. For each section, count the number of stomates that you see using the low-power lens.

- What is the average number of stomates that you observe?
- How can you determine the area that you see through the low-power lens? Once you have determined the area that is visible through the microscope, calculate the stomate density of a geranium leaf: that is, the number of stomates per unit area.
- What do you estimate is the total number of stomates on the geranium leaf? On the entire plant?
- Examine leaves from other plants. Do these plants have stomates on the surface of their leaves?
- Does stomate density seem to be relatively constant from plant to plant, or does it differ significantly with the species of plant?

GREENHOUSE GASES

There are a number of gases that can contribute to the global warming of the earth's surface and oceans. There are also a number of factors, such as volcanic eruptions, that can cause the earth's temperature to decrease. We can't help but wonder what overall effect these factors will have on global temperature in the near and distant future. For example, will increasing temperatures melt polar ice and cause oceans to rise sufficiently to submerge the great ocean ports of the world?

To analyze this problem thoroughly we would need to consider each of the possible causes of global warming. Then we would attempt to understand how all these factors affect each other to produce some net result. In this section, we will focus on only one of the factors related to global warming—carbon dioxide.

One well-known source of global warming is water

vapor in the atmosphere. Water molecules absorb infrared radiation. Without these molecules the earth would be considerably cooler than it is today. This heat absorption is often referred to as the "greenhouse effect." Other than water vapor, carbon dioxide is considered to be the most important contributor to the greenhouse effect. Other greenhouse gases include methane, chlorofluorocarbons, such as freon, and nitrous oxide.

- What are the natural and the man-made sources of carbon dioxide in the earth's atmosphere?

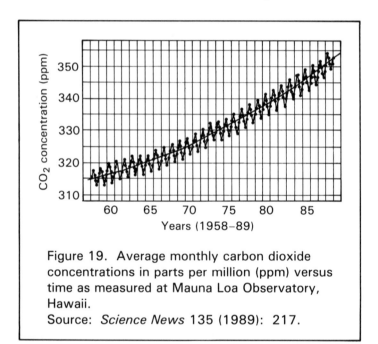

Figure 19. Average monthly carbon dioxide concentrations in parts per million (ppm) versus time as measured at Mauna Loa Observatory, Hawaii.
Source: *Science News* 135 (1989): 217.

Figure 19 is a graph of monthly average carbon dioxide concentrations in the atmosphere as measured at the summit of the Mauna Loa Observatory in Hawaii. Figure 20 is an expanded graph of carbon dioxide concentrations in the atmosphere for the year 1988.

- Describe the carbon dioxide concentration at the summit of Mauna Loa over the time period shown in Figure 19.
- Describe the annual month-to-month variation in carbon dioxide concentration shown in Figure 20.
- Can you explain the month-to-month variation by considering natural seasonal effects on carbon dioxide concentration?

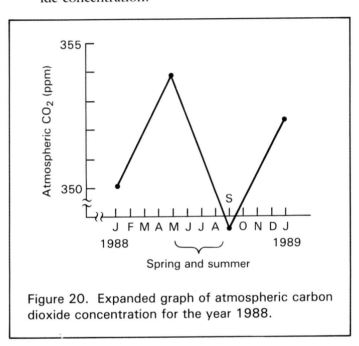

Figure 20. Expanded graph of atmospheric carbon dioxide concentration for the year 1988.

Finally, Figure 21 is an expanded graph showing carbon dioxide concentrations in the atmosphere for the years 1880 to 1989. The pre-1958 concentrations were determined by measuring the carbon dioxide found in ice cores. The concentration of the dissolved gas in the cores was carefully related to the Mauna Loa observations of atmospheric carbon dioxide in order to form a continuous scale.

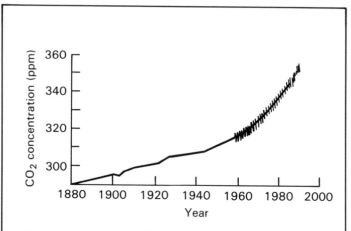

Figure 21. Carbon dioxide concentration from 1880 to 1989. The smooth portion of the curve was determined by measuring carbon dioxide in ice cores, and the remainder is from Fig. 19. Source: *Science News* 135 (1989): 215, 217.

- What do you conclude about the change in atmospheric carbon dioxide over the last hundred years of the industrial revolution? What is the percentage change in carbon dioxide concentration?
- What can you conclude about the effects of increased carbon dioxide in the atmosphere on global warming? Keep in mind that warming can take place in the atmosphere, on the earth's surface, and in the oceans.

GLOBAL WARMING

In the previous section you saw that there has been an increase in the amount of carbon dioxide in the atmosphere over the past 100 years. But can climate researchers connect the rising level of greenhouse gases with a warming of earth's climate now or in the future? How can a greenhouse warming of the climate be distinguished from natural warming, such as that caused by increased solar radiation? Indeed, what do we mean by "global warming"? Can we show any trend in global warming over periods of time that are meaningful?

We will begin with two global surface temperature studies. The first, a recent British study, includes both land and sea surface temperatures. The second, a record from the Goddard Institute for Space Studies, includes only land data. Figures 22*a* and *b* shows the results of the two studies in graphical form.

- What has been the globally averaged change in surface temperature in each study over the past 100 years?
- What has been the average rate of surface temperature rise, in degrees per year, over the past century?
- How did surface temperature change in the years from 1940 to 1972?
- How did carbon dioxide accumulation change in these same years? (See Figure 21.)
- If you had available to you *only* the data for the years 1940–1972, what would you conclude about the relationship between carbon dioxide accumulation and global surface temperature?

Since it seems prudent to look at data that cover a long period, as well as the detailed data of shorter periods, study Figure 23, a graph of the change in Antarctic temperatures over the past 15,000 years. The data were obtained by studying deuterium isotopes in an Antarctic ice core.

- What has been the maximum increase in Antarctic temperature in any continuous period of time?
- Over how long a period did this rise take place?
- What was the rate of temperature rise, measured in degrees per year, over this period?

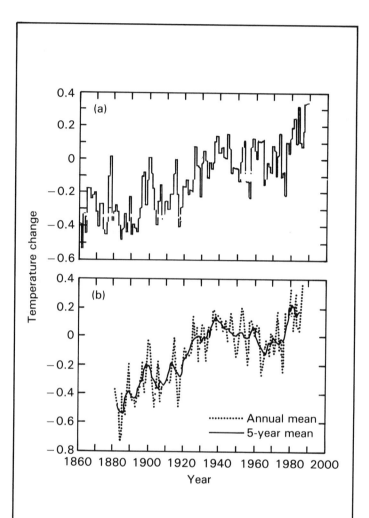

Figure 22. (a) Data from the United Kingdom Meteorological Office show temperature change over time for both land and ocean surfaces. (b) Data from the Goddard Institute for Space Sciences show temperature change for land only. Source: *Science News* 135 (1989): 216.

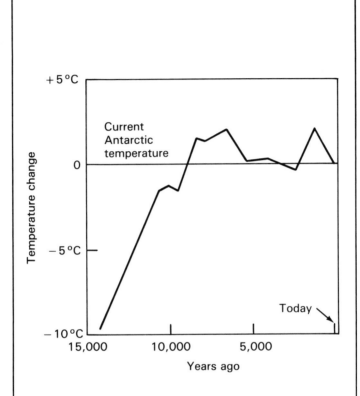

Figure 23. Changes in average Antarctic
temperature over the last 15,000 years.
Source: Adapted from Michael C. MacCracken,
ed., *Prospects for Future Climate*: *A Special
US/USSR Report on Climate Change*. Chelsea, Mi.:
Lewis, 1990.

- Compare this rate of rise with the estimated rate of surface temperature rise over the past century.

There are many possible reasons for global temperature change. Some of the most often cited reasons are: changes in solar radiation, impacts of asteroids with the earth, cataclysmic volcanic eruptions, changes in the earth's orbit around the sun, changes in the reflection of solar energy from the earth, accumulation of greenhouse gases such as carbon dioxide, increased atmospheric water vapor caused by a warming surface, and changes in continental plate tectonics causing changes in sea levels and ocean circulation.

- Which of these factors might cause global cooling? Which might cause global warming?
- Considering your answers to the previous question, can we be certain that the recent warming of the globe was caused by the greenhouse effect? Explain.

FOR FURTHER READING

Abrahamson, D.E., ed. *The Challenge of Global Warming*, Washington, D.C.: Island Press, 1985.

Ballard, Robert D. *Exploring Our Living Planet*, Washington, D.C.: National Geographic, 1988.

Ferris, Timothy. *Coming of Age in the Milky Way*. New York: Morrow, 1988.

Ferris, Timothy, ed. *The World Treasury of Physics, Astronomy, and Mathematics*. Boston: Little Brown, 1991.

Hopkins, Nigel J., Mayne, John W., and Hudson, John R. *The Numbers You Need*. Detroit: Gale Research, Inc., 1992.

Jacobs, Harold R. *Mathematics: A Human Endeavor*. New York: W. H. Freeman, 1982.

Judson, Horace F. *The Search for Solutions*. New York: Holt, 1980.

Stwertka, Albert. *Recent Revolutions in Mathematics*. New York: Watts, 1987.

Thomas, David A. *Math Projects for Young Scientists*. New York: Watts, 1988.

INDEX